ROAD TRIP

ROAD TRIP

A POCKET HISTORY OF INDIANA

BY ANDREA NEAL

INDIANA HISTORICAL SOCIETY PRESS
INDIANAPOLIS 2016

© 2016 Indiana Historical Society Press

This book is a publication of the
Indiana Historical Society Press
Eugene and Marilyn Glick Indiana History Center
450 West Ohio Street
Indianapolis, Indiana 45202-3269 USA
www.indianahistory.org
Telephone orders 1-800-447-1830
Fax orders 1-317-234-0562
Online orders @ http://shop.indianahistory.org

Printed in China

The paper in this publication meets the minimum requirements of American
National Standard for Information Sciences—Permanence of Paper for Printed
Library Materials, ANSI Z39. 48–1984 ∞

ISBN: 978-0-87195-395-7

TO MOM, DAD, AND DEDE
THREE OF THE PROUDEST
HOOSIERS I KNOW.

A MESSAGE FROM THE IHS PRESIDENT

In August 1915 author Theodore Dreiser and artist Franklin Booth, both Indiana natives, set off from New York City in a sixty-horsepower, Hoosier-made Pathfinder touring car on a trip that brought Dreiser home after a more than twenty-year absence. "It had been one of my dearly cherished ideas," Dreiser wrote, "that some day, when I had the time and the money to spare, I was going to pay a return visit to Indiana."

The result of the two-week, 2,000-mile journey was a book, *A Hoosier Holiday*, published in Indiana's 1916 centennial year. Dreiser's work helped inaugurate an era of "highway literature" or "road books," inspiring others to hit the road in their cars and visit long-forgotten destinations of their past.

It seems more than appropriate in 2016, to help commemorate the bicentennial of Indiana's statehood, that the Indiana Historical Society follow, as it were, in Dreiser's tire tracks by publishing Andrea Neal's *Road Trip: A Pocket History of Indiana*. Andrea's book is an open invitation for those who now live in the state, and Hoosiers from all over the country, to rediscover the historic sites and landmarks where Indiana history was made.

There is always, of course, more to learn about the nineteenth state's past. We encourage those who visit the one hundred locations in this book, and want to know more about Indiana's history, to visit the IHS's Destination Indiana online portal (http://www.destination-indiana.com/). Here you will discover stories from all of the state's ninety-two counties—one to five journeys for each one—and tales about African Americans, the Civil War, the Ohio River, mapping the state, social justice and reform, notable Hoosiers, art, literature, transportation, and agriculture. What is your 2016 destination?

Sincerely,

John A. Herbst

John A. Herbst
President and CEO
Indiana Historical Society

CONTENTS

PREFACE

As a teacher of U.S. history, I appreciate road trips. It is one thing to read about the War of 1812 in a textbook; it is another to walk across the field where William Henry Harrison's troops defeated The Prophet's forces at the Battle of Tippecanoe.

This book was designed to get Hoosiers to take road trips during the state's bicentennial. It is an effort to boil down centuries of history into bite-size stories reflecting the top 100 events, figures, and places every Indiana citizen should know.

From the beginning, I wanted to reach as many people as possible with these stories of our past, recognizing that few of us learned Indiana history beyond fourth grade, the age when it is taught in schools. Sad to say, we are woefully ignorant of our own story.

Craig Ladwig at the Indiana Policy Review Foundation, a nonprofit think tank headquartered in Fort Wayne, embraced the idea. He agreed to offer the column free of charge to his newspaper distribution list beginning in the summer of 2013. The material was not the foundation's typical fare, but Craig has always believed that good policy, regardless of politics, should be made only by those who know and understand their history.

Early reviews from readers were so encouraging that I approached Indiana Historical Society president and CEO John Herbst about the possibility of compiling the pieces into a book. To my delight, he and IHS Press senior director Ray E. Boomhower made it happen.

The biggest challenge was to narrow down the possible subjects to 100. At least half the topics were slam dunks, stories so significant that they would make any historian's list, such as the writing of Indiana's 1816 constitution, the removal of Native Americans from the "land of the Indians," and the wars that have been the constant theme of human history no matter the location.

For variety, I searched out less-familiar stories that deserve to be widely known, such as draining the Grand Kankakee Marsh and the role played by Hoosier Horace Hickam in the establishment of the U.S. Air Force.

One caveat was that every article had to have a destination attached: a museum, monument, county historical society, park, sculpture, or annual event that Hoosiers could attend or visit so that the history would come alive in their mind's eye. In some instances, I settled for historic markers when the landmark itself was no longer standing, for example at the site of the Dublin, Indiana, women's rights convention.

I began my stories during the Ice Age because that's how James H. Madison began his two definitive surveys of Indiana history: *The Indiana Way* (1986) and *Hoosiers: A New History of Indiana* (2014). Those two books were my most trusted advisers in the research and writing process.

I am thankful to attorney Ed Harris and my former newspaper colleague Kim Hooper, who did the legwork on several topics in their areas of expertise; to Laura Harris for her photographic skills at Columbus, Indiana, Wendell Willkie Park, and other spots that demanded an artistic eye; and to retired government and history teacher Tom Brogan, who accompanied me to many heritage sites referenced in this book. He and I were routinely amazed by destinations that we had no idea existed in our home state, despite a combined 110 years living here. On multiple occasions we walked away from a place saying, "Now *that's* the best-kept secret in Indiana."

For readers who intend to use this book as a travel guide, please go online or make a phone call to check directions, admission prices, and hours of operation before setting off on your own adventures. I discovered early in the process that some of the more unusual destinations are operated seasonally and/or by volunteers, and the operating hours change frequently.

I speak on behalf of all Hoosiers in expressing appreciation for the folks who keep those places running out of their deep love of Indiana and its heritage. May more Hoosiers come to their aid in coming years so that all the places I describe in this book are alive and well for the state's 250th birthday in 2066.

THE ICE AGE MADE MODERN INDIANA

Long before Indiana was Indiana, a river of ice glided across the state, bringing with it monsoon-like rains, mudflows to rival Mount Saint Helens, and rich sediment deposits that to this day nourish the crops that are the backbone of the Hoosier economy.

Indiana the state has been two hundred years in the making. Indiana the place goes back two million years to a time when ice sheets blanketed the middle latitudes and shaped the landscape we know today.

Virtually all aspects of modern Indiana were "in one way or another affected by some facet of the Ice Age," said geologist Anthony Fleming.

Consider the following: The rivers that attracted Native American settlements and later the pioneers, carried flatboats filled with trade goods, and powered gristmills and sawmills are former glacial rivers that drained the melting ice sheets.

Huge holes carved by advancing glaciers became the Great Lakes. These, along with the Saint Lawrence River, linked Indiana to the Atlantic Ocean and Europe.

Vast ice sheets deposited nutrient-rich soil and then flattened it, giving central and northern Indiana some of the nation's most productive farmland.

Aquifers formed during the Ice Age provide most of the water we need for household use and for industry.

To picture Indiana during the Ice Age, Hoosiers must set aside familiar images of forested wilderness and checkerboard farm fields. Instead, imagine a massive piece of ice molding the land like a potter modeling clay and ending where the hills of southern Indiana begin. Then imagine the ice's retreat, following by trickles then gushes of running water.

Scientists believe this pattern of gliding, melting, and receding ice happened at least three times in Indiana's ancient past. It is almost entirely responsible for the landscape of the northern two-thirds of the state. The geography of southern Indiana is due to bedrock, not glaciers.

Vestiges of the Ice Age can be seen all around, from the sand dunes of northern Indiana to the sandstone cliffs in the central part of the state. A striking example is Pine Hills Nature Preserve near Crawfordsville and adjacent to Shades State Park. Glacial melt water there formed two meandering streams (Clifty and Indian Creeks) that carved a deep gorge through bedrock and left four narrow ridges rising almost a hundred-feet tall. Over one ridge, the pathway is treacherous with a sheer drop-off on both sides. A short distance away, there is a massive wall of sandstone where the two creeks meet.

It is not the Grand Canyon, but it proves there is more to Indiana than flat farmland. Just look around. The Ice Age formed Indiana's landscape and its identity.

Directions to Pine Hills Nature Preserve: From I-74, head south on US 231 to Crawfordsville. From Crawfordsville, go south on Indiana 47 to Indiana 234. Go west on 234 about ten miles to entry of Shades State Park. Take the first right after the gatehouse to trailhead.

OPPOSITE: The trail over Devil's Backbone is six-feet wide with sheer drop-off on both sides.

MOUNDS LEAVE EVIDENCE
OF INDIGENOUS HOOSIERS

Indiana's name means "Land of the Indians." A trip to Mounds State Park in Anderson reminds us why.

Among the first inhabitants of our state were the Adena, a hunting-and-gathering people that lived in east central Indiana beginning around 1000 BC. They left behind earthen monuments—deep ditches surrounded by embankments—that offer clues to a complex society that understood astronomical events and seasonal calendars and based religious celebrations around them.

Visitors to Mounds State Park go to camp, hike, fish or swim. While there, most stand in awe at the ten mounds and earthworks ranging from a few inches to several feet high that have been on the National Register of Historic Places since 1973.

"The earthworks at Mounds State Park are some of the best protected of any in the state, and many improvements in protection have been instituted over the years," noted archeologist Donald Cochran, professor emeritus at Ball State University, who, with colleague Beth McCord, conducted much of the recent research there. "It is only one of five large earthwork complexes in east central Indiana. These five large sites, as well as many mounds and other enclosures, make up a cultural landscape that is unique in Indiana."

Although little is known about the daily lives of the Adena, their mounds and artifacts gave scholars enough data to generalize about these early Hoosiers. They were part of the Woodland Tradition that relied on hunting, fishing, berry picking, and cultivation of maize. They made ceramic pots and traded with other native peoples. When the Adena left they were replaced by the Hopewell, who used the mounds and constructed more for burial and ritual purposes. More than 300 of their ancient earthworks could once be found in east central Indiana, but today fewer than 100 remain.

Indiana is fortunate that Frederick Bronnenberg was the first private-property owner of the land that is now Mounds State Park. A native of Germany who immigrated to the United States around 1800, Bronnenberg protected the mounds from plowing and vandals.

Visitors on Trail 1 will discover the Great Mound, the largest and best preserved earthwork at Mounds State Park.

His son, Frederick Jr., did the same and "extolled their virtue as a community point of interest and destination," according to state park documents.

The area functioned from 1897 to 1929 as an amusement park that marketed the mounds as a tourist sight. The park shut down due to lagging attendance during the Great Depression and was sold to the Madison County Historical Society. The Society transferred ownership to the state in 1930, thus protecting the mounds from commercial and agricultural development—though not from public use or natural erosion.

State officials hope to implement more protective strategies in coming years. Their commitment is welcome and essential if Hoosiers are to preserve this vestige of prehistoric Indiana for future generations.

Directions to Mounds State Park: Approaching Anderson from the South on I-69, take exit 226. Turn left onto Indiana 9 North (South Scatterfield Road). Go about three miles then turn right on Mounds Road (Indiana 232). Mounds State Park will be on your left. $7 entry fee per vehicle.

INDIANA'S ECONOMY BUILT ON FARM FOUNDATION

By the time Europeans reached Indiana in the 1600s, our economic future was already set. Cornfields stretched for miles along the river valleys and colorful vegetables filled gardens tended by Native Americans. Indiana was destined to be an agricultural state. Climate and topography made it so.

In 1794, after General Anthony Wayne's army defeated Native Americans at the Battle of Fallen Timbers near Toledo, Ohio, Wayne's troops spent days destroying Indian grain fields throughout the Maumee River valley toward present-day Fort Wayne. One soldier told of maize plantations, bean patches, apple-tree stands, and potato plots. Wayne said he had never "beheld such immense fields of corn in any part of America, from Canada to Florida."

Ever since, farming has been the foundation of Indiana's economy. Nationally Indiana ranks fifth in corn, fifth in soybeans, and second in popcorn production.

"Agriculture's Bounty: The Economic Contribution of Agriculture," published by the Indiana Business Research Center, credits the agricultural sector for 190,000 Hoosier jobs. Of those, 103,000 are directly involved in crop production and processing.

It is no accident that Indiana is known for these things. The late Indiana University geographer Stephen Sargent Visher wrote in his 1944 book *Climate of Indiana*: "During about nine months in the year the temperatures are more favorable than prevail in most of the world." Long stretches between frosts, reliable rainfall, and warm summer days and nights create almost ideal farming conditions.

Scholars trace the genetic origins of corn back 10,000 years to a central American grass called teosinte, but it was the upper Mississippian Oneota peoples who lived along the Wabash River who became "the first fully adapted maize agriculturalists" according to one study of native activity in the late prehistoric period, 950 to 1650 AD.

It is a legacy passed down to modern farmers such as Joe Steinkamp of Evansville, Indiana, who farms the Ohio River bottoms.

"The neat thing about our climate is we have a nice long growing season, which gives us a bigger window to plant our crops," said

ABOVE: Corn nears maturity at a farm along Jordan Creek in Tippecanoe County. INSET: Joe Steinkamp of Evansville and his family grow white food-grade corn that is made into corn tortilla chips.

Steinkamp, whose land is about evenly divided between corn and soybeans. Unlike most Hoosier farmers who grow corn exclusively for animal feed, Steinkamp's is a white variety that is processed into Mexican-style dishes and tortilla chips.

Hoosiers can learn about the Steinkamps and other farm families at the Glass Barn at the Indiana State Fair. Sponsored by the Indiana Soybean Alliance, the facility is designed to educate Hoosiers about what life is like for farmers and their families. The building features interactive exhibitions, including a video theater where visitors can connect virtually with farmers. It is open daily throughout the fair's run in August and year-round for educational programs.

"We feel like the barn is an important step. We need to educate the Indiana consumer about what we are doing on the farm," said Kevin Wilson of Walton, Indiana, past alliance president and himself a corn and soybean farmer.

As the joke goes, "You know you're in Indiana when . . . all you see are corn and soybeans." There's more than a grain of truth to it. It's an important part of our history and our present.

Directions to the Glass Barn: The Glass Barn is open during the Indiana State Fair. It is adjacent to Pioneer Village on the north side of the Indiana State Fairgrounds in Indianapolis.

FIRST WHITE MAN IN INDIANA?
UN FRANCAIS, SANS DOUTE

Historians are not sure which white man stepped first on Hoosier soil, but he most certainly was French and he likely arrived in the 1670s—150 years before Indiana became the nineteenth state.

"Possibly it was an obscure Frenchman whose adventures were never recorded—if he lived to tell the tale," wrote historians John Barnhart and Dorothy Riker in *Indiana to 1816*, the first in a five-volume history published for the state's sesquicentennial in 1971.

Perhaps it was Jacques Marquette, the Jesuit priest sent to New France (now Canada) as missionary to the Indians. He explored the Mississippi River with Louis Jolliet and returned to northern Michigan possibly by way of northern Indiana in 1675.

Or it may have been René-Robert Cavelier, Sieur de La Salle, who set up camp at present-day South Bend in 1679 during a portage from the Saint Joseph River to the Kankakee River. LaSalle later explored the Mississippi River and claimed the surrounding land for France, dubbing it Louisiana in honor of the French king.

A historic marker installed in 1950 marks the spot one mile east of where LaSalle and his party camped overnight at South Bend. The marker declares LaSalle as "the first white man to enter Indiana," though subsequent scholarship has cast doubt on the claim, said former Indiana Historical Bureau director Pam Bennett.

The Bureau is in the process of updating the text on the oldest of its 500 markers. The revisions will reflect new research as well as more demanding standards for documentation of a subject's historic significance.

The LaSalle Camp marker is a mile east of where LaSalle and his party stayed in December 1679 on their portage from the Saint Joseph River to the Kankakee River. Text on the marker will eventually be revised to reflect uncertainty over whether the French explorer was the first white man in Indiana.

About one mile west of the LaSalle marker on Darden Road is a bridge, now used by pedestrians, that crosses the Saint Joseph River. It's near the likely campsite used by LaSalle and his men during their December 1679 portage. The bridge, previously called Four Mile Bridge, was built in 1885 by P. E. Lane of Chicago and is historic in its own right. The metal-truss highway bridge is on the National Register of Historic Places.

Another LaSalle marker installed in 2000 on the Kankakee River near the Starke County and La Porte County lines is less definitive. It describes the explorer's canoe trip "down the meandering Kankakee River through vast marsh-swamp-dune ecosystems which covered over 625 square miles and teemed with game including fish, waterfowl and mammals."

The portage route between the rivers stretched about four miles, crossing mostly prairie grass and woods. Long ago erased by farming and residential development, the trail was well known among seventeenth-century trappers who learned of it from Indian guides.

Because Jolliet placed the Saint Joseph River on a map in 1674, historians suspect he knew of the portage and may have chosen that route when he accompanied an ailing Marquette from Illinois back to the Great Lakes in 1675.

"The question of who was first may not ever be answered without qualification," Bennett said.

This much is definite. The French beat the English to Indiana—some of them merely passing through on their way elsewhere and others setting up forts or hunting for beaver in the lucrative fur trade. In the seventeenth and eighteenth centuries, France's North American empire stretched from Canada to the Gulf of Mexico, and two northern Indiana rivers held a strategic position.

Directions to LaSalle Camp marker in South Bend: From US 31, take Business 31, also called State Road 933, to the intersection with Darden Road. The marker is adjacent to a Key Bank branch at 19730 Darden Road.

LAND OF THREE RIVERS—FROM MIAMI CAPITAL TO FORT WAYNE

It is no coincidence that Indiana's second largest city occupies land that once served as a capital of the Miami Indian Nation. Native Americans chose Fort Wayne for its strategic location. The confluence of three rivers—the Saint Joseph, Saint Marys, and Maumee—proved equally appealing to French fur traders, English military men, and American pioneers.

"This area was important for one main reason," said Kathleen O'Connell, a volunteer for Historic Fort Wayne. "Three rivers converged at a point where there was a short portage of six to nine miles to another series of rivers that would ultimately take you all the way to the Gulf of Mexico."

Historic Fort Wayne is a not-for-profit group that manages the Old Fort, a replica of the last active fort in the Three Rivers Area. It is located near the original Miami village of Kekionga. James Madison, in his book *The Indiana Way*, described Kekionga as "the meeting ground of the Miami tribal council" and "one of the most significant strategic locations in the trans-Appalachian West."

The French arrived at Kekionga in the late seventeenth century and built a fortified trading post as a way to lay claim to the region. A series of forts followed. The first was built between 1712 and 1722 adjacent to the Saint Marys River near where the portage trail began. It was known by different names: Saint Phillipe, Post Miami, or Fort Miami. It was primarily a trading post for the fur traders but also a base for French soldiers.

During the 1730s and 1740s, the British, seeking to share in the profits from the fur trade by eliminating French competition, gained the support of the local Indians, who burned Fort Miami in 1747. Three years later, the French rebuilt the fort at a new location on the east side of the Saint Joseph River. In 1760, at the end of the French and Indian War, this fort was surrendered to the British. Native forces destroyed it in 1763 during Pontiac's Rebellion, a major uprising against the British. General Anthony Wayne established the first

Reenactors greet visitors to Historic Fort Wayne, a replica of the last active fort in the Three Rivers area. The fort is based on drawings by Major John Whistler, who oversaw its construction in 1816.

American fort on the site in 1794. A new structure was built in 1798, and it proved pivotal during the War of 1812, turning back repeated assaults by heavily armed Indians. In 1816 Major John Whistler oversaw construction of the last active military fort. His drawings were the basis for the replica that opened in 1976 to celebrate the nation's bicentennial.

"I think it's often hard to get people excited about history," O'Connell said. "When history jumps off the page of a book and comes alive, it makes a huge difference—both in learning and caring about our past, and our commitment to preserve it."

Directions to Old Fort Wayne: Address is 1201 Spy Run Avenue. From I-69 take the Jefferson Boulevard exit toward downtown Fort Wayne, merging onto West Jefferson Boulevard. Continue for about seven miles and then turn left on Lafayette Street/US 27 North. Parking is available on Fourth Street between Spy Run Avenue and Clinton Street or at Headwaters Park across the river.

ON THE BANKS OF THE WABASH HISTORY HAPPENED

Storied in literature and song, the Wabash is Indiana's most important river. It is the official river of the state of Indiana, so designated by law in 1996. It is the subject of the state song, "On the Banks of the Wabash, Far Away," written by Paul Dresser in 1897. It is referred to in the state poem as "the dreamy Wabash River."

The Wabash's significance goes beyond aesthetics; it played a key role in trade, transportation, and military tactics even before Indiana became a state. "Much of the struggle for control of the New World by the French and British took place along the Wabash," according to the Indiana Department of Natural Resources.

Wabash is the English version of the name given the river by the Miami Indians who lived in its upper valley near Fort Wayne. Their word—Wah-bah-shik-ki—means pure white water, a reference to the white limestone bed stretching from the river's source near Fort Recovery, Ohio, to Logansport, Indiana.

The French Jesuits, earliest visitors to the region, spelled it Ouabache, thus the spelling of Ouabache State Park in Wells County, whose southern edge runs along the river east of Bluffton.

British lieutenant governor Edward Abbott, posted at Vincennes during the American Revolution, wrote this about the river in 1777: "The Wabache is perhaps one of the finest rivers in the world; on its banks are several Indian towns, the most considerable is the Ouija, where it is said there are 1,000 men capable to bear arms."

He was referring to the Wea band of Miami, who had migrated from the Great Lakes to the banks of the Wabash near West Lafayette. The Wea grew maize, melons, and pumpkins and traded with other tribes up and down the river.

In 1717 the French selected the north bank of the Wabash, directly across from the Wea village, to build a fortified post to deter British settlement and facilitate fur trade. From 1720 to 1760, Fort Ouiatenon (wee-ah-tuh-gnaw) flourished. One visitor described it as "the finest palisaded fort in the upper country, consisting of a stockade and a double row of houses."

Historic Fort Ouiatenon Park is about one mile from the site of the original French post built in 1717. INSET: *This view looks across the Wabash River from Historic Fort Ouiatenon Park to the probable location of the Wea village.*

A replica of the blockhouse was built in 1930 and is open to visitors on weekends from 1:00 p.m. to 5:00 p.m. May through September. Each year the site hosts the Feast of the Hunters' Moon, a reenactment of the annual fall gathering that brought together French and Native Americans. (For more information, see http://www.tcha.mus .in.us/feast.htm.)

After the Indians were pushed out of the state in the nineteenth century, the Wabash continued to play a vital role. It was a major route west taken by pioneers. The Wabash-Erie Canal was built along it and gave farmers access to markets in the East until canals were made obsolete by railroads.

Except for thirty of its five hundred miles, the Wabash is an Indiana river, forming two hundred miles of the state's boundary with Illinois.

Today the river offers water supply and recreational opportunities, but it can no longer be called pure white. Runoff from farmland has turned it muddy brown as it moves slowly but surely toward its confluence with the Ohio River below Mount Vernon, Indiana.

Directions to Fort Ouiatenon: The street address is 3129 South River Road, West Lafayette, IN 47906. From I-65, take the Indiana 26 exit. Turn left on Indiana 26 West and continue to follow it to South River Road/US 231. Turn left and go about four miles.

BISON MIGRATING WEST CREATED FIRST INDIANA ROAD

Bison made Indiana's first highway. It started at the Falls of the Ohio near modern-day Clarksville, Indiana, where the beasts came together to cross the Ohio River at its shallowest point. It ended near Vincennes, where they scattered to graze on Illinois prairie grass.

If you look closely, you can still see signs of the Buffalo Trace. "You kind of have to know what you're looking for," said Teena Ligman, public affairs specialist for the U.S. Forest Service. She described the remnants as trail beds or trenches that, to an untrained eye, might appear the work of human labor rather than hooves.

Archeologists are not sure exactly when the trail appeared, but they suspect thousands of bison traversed it during their seasonal migration from Kentucky salt licks to feeding grounds on the prairie. The trail's width ranged from twelve to twenty feet across.

The 1910 book *Early Indiana Trails and Surveys* by George R. Wilson put the matter in historic perspective: "The trails and traces were great highways over which civilization came into the wilderness. Wild animals often followed the trails, trappers followed the game, and settlers followed the trappers."

It's fitting that the buffalo (more accurately called bison) is featured so prominently on Indiana's state seal. Until 1800 or so, bison were abundant over large portions of what became the Indiana Territory and the state of Indiana.

In 1720 the historian Charlevoix, who had traveled extensively in New France and across the Great Lakes region, wrote, "All the country that is watered by the Oaubache [Wabash], and by the Ohio which runs into it, is very fruitful. It consists of vast meadows, well watered, where the wild buffalo feed by thousands."

Settlers mistook the animals for buffalo because they looked so much alike, but it was a misnomer; the American bison is a distant relative.

Surveyors in the 1800s often drew the Trace and adjacent buffalo wallows on Indiana maps. A 1910 history of Dubois County by Wilson described the wallow remnants as "big circular patches, where the grass was greener, thicker and higher than anywhere else around."

Wallows were essentially huge mud puddles dug out by bison in order to take cooling baths.

Although the bison disappeared, their route was put to good use. Archeologists believe it served as a trade route for Native Americans. Pioneers followed it west. In the early nineteenth century, a stagecoach line ran the length of the Trace from New Albany to Vincennes. Much of it was eventually paved over as US 150.

Today, there's scant evidence of the Trace. There is a spot off State Road 37, about six miles south of Paoli, where motorists can see trenches in both directions. Probably the best way to experience the Trace is on the Springs Valley Trail in the Hoosier National Forest southeast of French Lick. A segment of the trail follows the Trace, and attentive hikers may notice other remnants and signs of wallows from centuries ago.

Directions to Springs Valley Trailhead: From French Lick, take Indiana 145 south for 6.4 miles, then turn left at the Forest Service sign on Baseline Liberty Road.

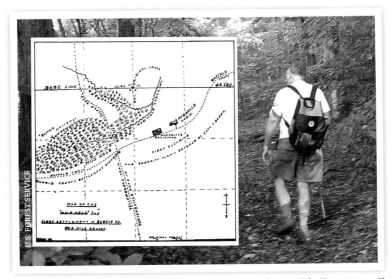

ABOVE: *A hiker follows a short surviving section of the Buffalo Trace just off the main path of the Springs Valley Trail in the Hoosier National Forest.* INSET: *The Buffalo Trace and a mud hole as they were mapped and described in the original 1805 land survey of Dubois County, Indiana.*

FIRST CHURCH CONGREGATION STILL THRIVING IN VINCENNES

Roman Catholics claim bragging rights to Indiana's oldest church. Jesuit missionaries visited the French fort at Vincennes within months of its establishment in 1732. A resident priest, Sebastian Meurin, arrived in 1748. People have been worshipping at Saint Francis Xavier Church ever since.

"If the French built a fort, there was a chapel," said the Reverend John Schipp, parish priest at the Old Cathedral for many years. "They not only wanted to trade, they wanted to invite the natives to become Christians."

Scholars agree the Jesuits were first to bring Christ to what is now Indiana. Founded in 1540 by Saint Ignatius Loyola, the Society of Jesus is an order of priests whose primary mission field at that time was pagan lands.

Whenever the French built a military or trading post in the New World, a church followed. Unlike the Protestant churches built by later pioneers, who focused on moral and social needs of their immediate communities, the Jesuits' concern was outward.

"The records of St. Francis Xavier's church . . . show from April 1749, and for a half century after, the greater part of the entries of baptisms, marriages and funerals were of Indian converts," noted the *History of Old Vincennes and Knox County, Indiana* by George E. Greene.

Although the church today has stable membership of 350 households, its beginnings were rocky, reflecting the political turbulence of the times. When the area came under British control in 1763 at the end of the French and Indian War, the Jesuits were expelled and the congregation relied on lay leadership for two decades, noted Richard Day, congregation historian. During that time, the Illinois-based Reverend Pierre Gibault traveled to Vincennes to check on the parish. Day told of a visit in 1769 when Gibault was "greeted by a desperate crowd crying, 'Save us, Father; we are nearly in hell!'"

During the American Revolution, Gibault sided with the rebels. On July 20, 1778, he persuaded the people of Vincennes to pledge loyalty to the United States and to turn over their fort to George Rogers Clark. Gibault assumed leadership of the parish after the war.

A bronze statue of Gibault, "Patriot Priest of the Old Northwest," stands in front of the church to mark his role in the capture of the Northwest Territory from the British. In 1970 Pope Paul VI elevated the church to the rank of basilica due to its religious and historic significance.

The parish's earliest written record is from April 21, 1749. Its first building was a log shelter with bark roof, replaced twice before the current red brick structure went up in 1826.

Located steps from the George Rogers Clark National Historical Park, the church is open daily for self-guided tours and for group tours by appointment with the Vincennes/Knox County Convention and Visitors Bureau (800-886-6443). Next to the church is the French and Indian Cemetery, which contains mostly unmarked graves of four thousand residents of early Vincennes.

Directions to Saint Francis Xavier Church: The address of the Old Cathedral Complex is 205 Church Street, Vincennes, IN 47591. From I-70, take the US 150/U.S. 41 Exit south to Vincennes. Continue onto US 41 Business and turn right on Church Street.

Statues of Saints Joan of Arc, Francis Xavier and Patrick adorn the niches in the face of the Old Cathedral in Vincennes.

REVOLUTIONARY HERO
GEORGE ROGERS CLARK

If not for George Rogers Clark, Hoosiers might snack on scones with jam and clotted cream and speak with Cockney accents.

An exaggeration perhaps, but as Kelley Morgan pointed out, "George Rogers Clark was almost singlehandedly responsible for the United States gaining the Old Northwest Territory."

Morgan is interpretive manager at Falls of the Ohio State Park in Clarksville, Indiana, where a representation of Clark's retirement home overlooks the falls with stunning views of the Ohio River.

A native of Tennessee, Morgan was unfamiliar with Clark until coming to Indiana, and she laments so few Americans know about his story. "I think George ended up being overshadowed by his younger brother William" of Lewis and Clark fame, she noted.

George Clark was born in 1752 in Virginia and was a lifelong friend of President Thomas Jefferson, with whom he shared passions for science, zoology, and Native Americans.

At the age of twenty, Clark went west on a surveying trip and claimed land for himself and friends in what became Kentucky. Life was tense there due to constant warfare with Native Americans and British laws against westward migration. In June 1776 his fellow citizens asked Clark to lobby the state of Virginia for military assistance and stronger political ties.

The charismatic redhead proved persuasive. Although preoccupied with the coming war for independence, Virginia granted Kentucky status as a county and five hundred pounds of gunpowder.

By 1777 Clark realized that the British were inciting Native American harassment of settlers, including paying bounties for prisoners and scalps. The Virginia legislature granted Clark a commission as lieutenant colonel and gave him permission to gather troops. Clark set his sights on capturing British forts in the Old Northwest, the territory that became Ohio, Indiana, Illinois, Michigan and Wisconsin.

Virginia governor Patrick Henry authorized Clark to attack the British fort of Kaskaskia (Illinois) in French-occupied territory on the

OPPOSITE: This monument at Vincennes commemorates the taking of Fort Sackville from the British in 1779.

George Rogers Clark's original two-room cabin was destroyed in 1854. This representation overlooks the Ohio River at Falls of the Ohio State Park.

Mississippi River. Clark set up a supply base at the Falls of the Ohio.

Clark and his men surprised Kaskaskia on July 4, 1778, taking the fort and town without firing a shot. In coming months, Clark rallied support from the French while planning another bold move against the British at Fort Sackville in Vincennes.

"On February 23, they surprised Vincennes," according to an Indiana Historical Bureau account. "Clark ordered that all of the company's flags be marched back and forth behind a slight rise to convince the British that there were 600 men rather than under 200. They opened fire on the fort with such accuracy that the British were prevented from opening their gun ports."

British officer Henry Hamilton surrendered on February 25 in the mistaken belief his side was overpowered. After Clark's victory, British influence on the frontier weakened. When the Treaty of Paris was signed in 1783 ending the American Revolution, the British ceded the entire Northwest Territory to the United States.

Clark spent much of his personal fortune on the war effort and was never repaid; he died in poverty and obscurity. His heroism is appropriately remembered at Clarksville and at Vincennes, where the National Park Service operates a memorial in his honor.

Directions to Falls of the Ohio State Park: Street address is 201 West Riverside Drive, Clarksville, Indiana. Take Exit 1 on I-65 and follow the signs.

Directions to George Rogers Clark National Historical Site: Street address is 401 South Second Street, Vincennes, Indiana. From I-70, go south on US 41 and follow the signs.

HOOSIER VALUES SHAPED BY THE NORTHWEST ORDINANCE

Indiana became a state in 1816. Its political values, moral compass, and physical boundaries were shaped by the Northwest Ordinance of 1787.

The ordinance spelled out how new states would be added to the Union and the rights that would be guaranteed to citizens. John J. Patrick, professor emeritus of education at Indiana University, called the ordinance "a brilliant policy for governing a vast area north and west of the Ohio River—a liberal and innovative plan for colonial administration and national development." The document "is indisputably at the core of the American civic heritage, one of the most important political legacies we have," Patrick added.

When the United States won the American Revolution, the thirteen original states gained massive new lands stretching west to the Mississippi River and north to the Great Lakes. The Northwest Ordinance was one of several laws passed by the national Congress governing land division and westward migration.

It dealt specifically with the Old Northwest—the Midwest today—out of which "not less than three nor more than five States" were to be carved. The result? Ohio (1803), Indiana (1816), Illinois (1818), Michigan (1837), and Wisconsin (1848).

The ordinance set forth a process by which territories would elect legislatures, write constitutions, and apply to the national government for statehood. It guaranteed new states would enter the union "on an equal footing with the original states" and specified their probable geographic borders.

The Ohio River became Indiana's southern boundary. The northern perimeter was a moving target for decades. After Ohio was admitted to the Union in 1803 and the Michigan Territory created in 1805, the boundary line was set at the southern tip of Lake Michigan. In 1816 the line was shifted ten miles further north so Indiana could claim a bit of lakeshore.

The governance procedures set forth in the ordinance were as far-sighted as its commitment to individual dignity. Consider the following enlightened promises.

Freedom of religion: "No person . . . shall ever be molested on account of his mode of worship or religious sentiments."

Education: "Religion, morality, and knowledge, being necessary to good government and the happiness of mankind, schools and the means of education shall forever be encouraged."

Respect of Native Americans: "The utmost good faith shall always be observed towards the Indians; . . . in their property, rights, and liberty, they shall never be invaded or disturbed."

Sad to say, the promises were not always kept. Throughout the Northwest Territory, federal treaties stripped Native Americans of their homeland, and slavery existed despite the written ban. The 1800 federal census recorded 135 slaves in the Indiana Territory and 163 free blacks. Regular funding for public schools did not occur until after the mid-nineteenth century.

Patrick lamented that the typical high school textbook contains less than a page on the Northwest Ordinance, calling it a seminal document in American history. Many of its principles made their way into the Indiana Constitution of 1816. Though the ordinance was superseded by other laws, Hoosiers can take pride in its formative influence.

Directions to Indiana Territory Boundary Line marker: Street address is 213 Pine Lake Avenue, La Porte, Indiana.

This La Porte County marker designates the Indiana Territory's northern border as of 1805 when the Michigan Territory was created.

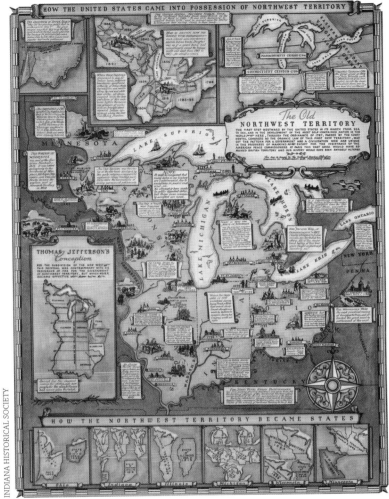

A 1937 map issued by the Northwest Territory Celebration Commission outlining how the United States obtained the territory and how each territory became a state.

LITTLE TURTLE LED IN WAR AND PEACE

For thirty years he was a dominating figure on the Indiana frontier, at first resisting the white man's encroachment and later giving in to the inevitable. The historian Calvin Young called him "one of the greatest Indian chiefs of all time."

"Some day we will recognize him as our first great Hoosier and an American of national importance," wrote Otho Winger, historian and Manchester College president, in 1942.

Indeed, Miami chief Little Turtle's name ranks with Abraham Lincoln and Benjamin Harrison as a figure all Hoosiers should recognize. He died four years before Indiana statehood, so there is no way to know if Little Turtle himself would have embraced the title, "first great Hoosier," or dismissed it as patronizing.

Known by his people as Me-she-kin-no-quah, Little Turtle was born on the banks of the Eel River about five miles east of modern-day Columbia City. A historic marker at the site lists his birth year as "c. 1747."

When the American Revolution ended in 1783, Great Britain ceded to the new United States the territory northwest of the Ohio River, including present-day Indiana. Immediately white settlers poured in.

Little Turtle organized a confederation of tribes—including Miami, Potawatomi, and Delaware—that for a time seemed capable of resisting pioneer migration into their hunting grounds. "He fought back against them in the only way he knew how," Winger wrote. "With small bodies of Indian warriors gathered from along [the] Eel River and the Wabash [River] he would make raids along the Ohio [River]."

This frontier violence was one of George Washington's thorniest problems when he became president in 1789. In 1790 he assigned General Josiah Harmar to capture the Miami capital at Kekionga near present-day Fort Wayne. Little Turtle's men stopped Harmar in his tracks. A year later, General Arthur Saint Clair led two thousand soldiers against the natives in western Ohio; he suffered one of the worst defeats in U.S. military history.

OPPOSITE: The Treaty of Greenville was a key event in Native American-U.S. government relations. Events leading up to it are described in a second-floor exhibition at the Eiteljorg Museum of American Indians and Western Art in Indianapolis.

1795: First Major Land Loss

You take too much of [our] lands away.... The print of my ancestors' houses are every where to be seen in this portion.

— Miami Chief Little Turtle, 1795

1795: Treaty of Greenville

Following the Battle of Fallen Timbers, the tribes are forced into negotiations leading to the Treaty of Greenville. More than 1,100 Indians representing 11 tribal groups assembled on the treaty grounds in western Ohio. It was the first significant loss of lands for the tribes of this area.

Do not deceive us in the manner that the French, the British and the Spaniards have heretofore done.
— Potawatomi Chief New Corn to General Wayne, 1795

...The United States relinquish their claims to all other Indian lands northward of the river Ohio, eastward of the Mississippi, and westward and southward of the Great Lakes. ...
— 1795 Treaty of Greenville

Little Turtle speaks privately to Wayne during treaty negotiations.
(The unknown artist of this oil painting is believed to have been a member of General Anthony Wayne's staff.)

In 1787, the U. S. Constitution states that the Congress has the power to regulate commerce with Indian Tribes and that the President shall have the power, with the "Advice and Consent of the Senate, to make Treaties."

Just as the U.S. deals with foreign nations, it deals with tribes.

The next time, Washington directed General Anthony Wayne to lead an expedition and persuaded Congress to provide him with enough arms and soldiers. Wayne spent the winter of 1793 near Greenville, Ohio, drilling his army for battle. Little Turtle spied on the activities and concluded the natives stood no chance against "a general who never sleeps." He advised fellow Indians to make peace, but the confederation council disagreed, and Little Turtle gave up his command.

The Battle of Fallen Timbers in August 1794 destroyed the confederation. Little Turtle and other chiefs signed the Treaty of Greenville that allowed Americans to settle peacefully into Ohio and Indiana. Hoosiers can learn more about this chapter in Indiana history at the Eiteljorg Museum of American Indians and Western Art in Indianapolis.

Little Turtle died in Fort Wayne in 1812 and was remembered with affection by U.S. political leaders. To others, however, his acceptance of federal policy toward Native Americans was seen as a sellout.

Historian Winger took the former view: "He already had the record of defeating more American armies than any other Indian chief. He was now to acquire the greater reputation of being most interested in ways of peace and civilization."

Directions to Eiteljorg Museum: Street address is 500 West Washington Street, Indianapolis, at the intersection of West and Washington Streets.

WILLIAM HENRY HARRISON SHAPED INDIANA FROM VINCENNES

History remembers William Henry Harrison as the first president to die in office. Hoosiers should remember him as the man who shaped the Indiana Territory.

Indiana spent sixteen years as a territory before it became a full-fledged state. Following a multistep process set out in the Northwest Ordinance, citizens first had to get practice at governing, grow in population, petition for statehood, be accepted into the Union, and write a constitution.

Like a conductor directing an orchestra, Harrison oversaw much of the process from his governor's mansion in Vincennes, the territorial capital chosen because it had a sizable population and was conveniently located on the Wabash River. In the process, he negotiated ten treaties with Native Americans, bringing the land firmly under U.S. control.

The Indiana Territory was much larger than what eventually became the state of Indiana. Carved out of the Northwest Territory in 1800, the Indiana Territory included Indiana, Illinois, Wisconsin, and parts of Minnesota and Michigan. At the time, some 12,000 Native Americans and 6,000 settlers lived there. By 1816 Indiana had been whittled down to its current size and had 64,000 residents.

Harrison, a native Virginian and a military man, was named territorial governor by President John Adams in 1800. Harrison moved to Vincennes in January 1801 and got to work writing laws, appointing public officials, improving roads, and directing Indian affairs.

In 1804 Harrison built a governor's residence sturdy enough to function as a fort. It was the first brick home in Indiana and became known as Grouseland due to abundant game birds in the area.

As the pursuit of statehood progressed, power shifted away from the executive, Harrison, to a democratic legislative branch. In 1811 the legislature asked Congress for permission to write a state constitution and admission to the Union. By this time, the territory hoped to be financially self-sufficient. It was not yet, so plans were put on hold. War broke out, and statehood was further delayed.

William Henry Harrison built this Georgian/Federal house in 1804, while serving as governor of the Indiana Territory. He named it Grouseland for the many game birds on the 300-acre property.

In the War of 1812 Harrison served as commander of the Northwest Army and resigned his post to concentrate on battling the British. In 1813 President James Madison appointed Thomas Posey as Harrison's replacement. That same year the legislature passed the State Capital Act, moving the territorial capital to Corydon, which would become the new state capital.

In 1815 the assembly again petitioned Congress for statehood, and this time all went according to plan. In December 1816 President James Madison signed a resolution admitting Indiana as the nineteenth state.

For the twelve years he served as governor, Harrison was synonymous with the Indiana Territory, and Grouseland functioned as the White House of the West. Today the mansion appears much as it did in the early nineteenth century and is "a cultural treasure in Indiana," noted historian James Fadely. "It embodies the history and culture of the early Indiana Territory within its walls."

Of the four meeting places of the legislature, one still stands: a two-story red house initially built as a tailor shop. The sites are within a block of each other and open to the public as living reminders of Indiana's beginnings.

Directions to Grouseland and Vincennes State Historic Sites: From I-70, take US 41 south to Vincennes. Turn right on Scott Street.

OPPOSITE: The second session of the Third General Assembly of the Indiana Territory met in this building in 1811. Of the four Vincennes meeting places of the territorial legislature, this is the only one that survived.

LEWIS AND CLARK JOINED FORCES IN INDIANA

In 1803 President Thomas Jefferson asked Meriwether Lewis to lead an exploration of the Louisiana Territory in search of a Northwest Passage. Lewis invited William Clark to join him. It became one of the most famous partnerships in history, and it started in Indiana.

"When they shook hands, the Lewis and Clark expedition began," wrote Stephen Ambrose in *Undaunted Courage*, the best-selling account of the transcontinental journey. Lewis was working at that time as Jefferson's private secretary in Washington, D.C. Clark was living with his brother, George Rogers Clark, in Clarksville in the Indiana Territory.

The two met up in Clarksville on October 14, 1803, and used the Clark cabin overlooking the Falls of the Ohio River as base camp while making final preparations. On October 26 the duo and their initial crew members pushed off down the Ohio River in a keelboat and red canoe and headed west to Saint Charles, Missouri, the expedition's official starting point.

"In practical terms the partnership of Lewis and Clark may be said to have begun during a 13-day interlude before they set out on Oct. 26," says Stephenie Ambrose Tubbs, author of *The Lewis and Clark Companion*.

Clark recruited the nucleus of the Corps of Discovery from the area around Clarksville and Louisville after being directed by Lewis "to find out and engage some good hunters, stout, healthy, unmarried men, accustomed to the woods, and capable of bearing bodily fatigue in a pretty considerable degree."

One of those recruits was Sergeant Charles Floyd, after whom Floyd County is named. Floyd lived in Clarksville and was the first constable of Clarksville Township. His death on August 20, 1804, near Sioux City, Iowa, likely from a ruptured appendix, was the only fatality among the thirty-three members in the "Permanent Party" of the 1804 to 1806 expedition.

OPPOSITE: *Montana artist Carol Grende sculpted lifelike figures of Meriwether Lewis and William Clark for the 2003 bicentennial celebration of the Lewis and Clark Expedition. The statue is at the entry to the Falls of the Ohio State Park.*

Two other members of the expedition had Indiana connections. Private John Shields was the oldest enlisted man at age thirty-four and a friend of Daniel Boone. His skills as a blacksmith and gunsmith were considered critical to the trip's success. Afterward he settled near Corydon. He died in 1809 and was buried in Little Flock Cemetery in Harrison County.

William Bratton was a skilled hunter who moved to Indiana after the expedition and became active in military and government affairs. By 1822 Bratton and his wife lived in Waynetown and had ten children. In 1824 he was appointed justice of the peace in Wayne Township and served as a local school superintendent. He died in 1841 and was buried in the Old Pioneer Cemetery in Montgomery County.

Indiana's role in the expedition is often overlooked by historians, though Clark's cabin and the crew's departure site are popular attractions for Lewis and Clark enthusiasts. The Falls of the Ohio State Park in Clarksville has an interpretive center where visitors can learn not only about Lewis and Clark but also the Devonian fossil beds exposed at the riverbank.

The park entry features ten-foot bronze figures of Lewis and Clark mounted on a sixteen-and-a-half-ton slab of Indiana limestone. The sculpture depicts the moment when Lewis and Clark greeted each other in Clarksville to begin their 8,000-mile trek.

Directions to Falls of the Ohio State Park: Take Exit 1 on Interstate 65 and follow the signs to 201 West Riverside Drive, Clarksville, Indiana.

SWISS CREATED EARLY COMMERCIAL WINERY IN INDIANA

In 1796 John James Dufour left his native Switzerland to seek a new life and opportunity in the United States. Less than a decade later, in southeastern Indiana, he opened the country's first successful winemaking business.

It was still the Indiana Territory at that time, but the settlement soon became the town of Vevay in Switzerland County. It was briefly a popular destination for Swiss immigrants fleeing revolutionary Europe.

Dufour had done his homework. As a teen, he studied viticulture and worked the family vineyards in Canton de Vaud, Switzerland. Upon his arrival in America, he visited private vineyards, including Thomas Jefferson's at Monticello, to study grape types, soil, and climate.

In an 1826 book detailing his experiences as a vintner, Dufour recalled the time he resolved to come to America:

> I was but 14; and I came to this determination by reading the newspapers, which were full of the American Revolutionary War and contained many letters from the officers of the French army aiding the republicans, which complained of the scarcity of the wine among them, in the midst of the greatest abundance of everything else. . . . By inspection of the maps, I saw that America was in the parallel of the best wine countries in the world—like Spain, south of France, Italy and Greece.

Dufour initially settled near Lexington, Kentucky, and was joined by extended family members. There they planted thirty-five grape varieties, most of which fell victim to disease because they were European species not suited to American growing conditions.

Uncomfortable with legal slavery in Kentucky, the family moved to Indiana and tried again, dubbing the area "New Switzerland" and this time focusing on the two grape varieties that had flourished in Kentucky: Cape and Madeira.

Congress in 1802 granted 2,500 acres to Dufour on credit, and he later bought 1,200 more for the community's expanding vineyards. He resold parcels to other French-speaking Swiss, including Louis Gex Oboussier, who purchased a tract of 319 acres along Indian Creek renamed Venoge by the Swiss after a river in their native land. The first wine was produced in 1806 or 1807 and sold in frontier cities including Cincinnati, Louisville, and Saint Louis.

Wine historians generally credit DuFour with establishing the first commercially successful vineyard, although Peter Legaux and the Pennsylvania Vine Company had been attempting to do so since the 1790s.

In the end, DuFour's business did not prove economically viable. It was eclipsed by hay, which was in high demand as livestock feed and easy to load onto riverboats passing through Vevay on their way down the Ohio River.

Although slated to be burned down in the mid-1990s, local preservationists stepped in to save the Musée de Venoge, and today it stands as a testament to southern Indiana's once thriving grape culture. The farmhouse dates to about 1815 and is a rare surviving example of the French colonial architecture that was used often by the French-Swiss immigrants.

The home is open Sundays from 1:00 p.m. to 4:00 p.m. from spring through fall and by appointment by calling (812) 593-5726. Although the grape vines are gone, the landscape is unchanged from the days of Dufour, Oboussier, and their fellow Swiss vine growers.

Directions to Musée de Venoge: From I-74, go south on Indiana 129 to Indian Creek one mile north of the Ohio River.

PHOTO BY DONNA WEAVER

The restored Venoge cottage reflects the French colonial style favored by Swiss grape growers in southeastern Indiana.

THE

AMERICAN

VINE-DRESSER'S GUIDE,

BEING A TREATISE

ON THE

CULTIVATION OF THE VINE,

AND

THE PROCESS OF WINE MAKING;

ADAPTED TO THE SOIL AND CLIMATE

OF THE

UNITED STATES:

BY JOHN JAMES DUFOUR,

FORMERLY OF SWISSERLAND, AND NOW AN AMERICAN CITIZEN;
CULTIVATOR OF THE VINE FROM HIS CHILDHOOD, AND FOR THE
LAST TWENTY FIVE YEARS, OCCUPIED IN THAT LINE OF
BUSINESS, FIRST IN ———, AND NOW ON THE
BORDERS OF OHIO, NEAR VEVAY, INDIANA.

Then said the trees to the vine, come thou, and reign over us.
And the vine said unto them, should I leave my wine, which cheer-
eth God and man, and go to be promoted over the trees?
Judges, c. ix. 12 & 13 vv.

Cincinnati:

PRINTED BY S. J. BROWNE,
AT THE EMPORIUM OFFICE.
....
1826.

---

*In 1826 John James Dufour compiled his wine knowledge into a textbook,
which compared American and European vineyards and advised "judicious
application of good manure" as prerequisite for a successful grape harvest.*

TIPPECANOE A TURNING POINT IN U.S.– NATIVE AMERICAN RELATIONS

In the drizzling predawn rain of November 7, 1811, on high ground near modern-day Lafayette, Indiana, General William Henry Harrison squashed Tecumseh's dream of an Indian confederacy that could resist the white man's westward advances.

The Battle of Tippecanoe was a defining moment in U.S.–Native American relations. "It was on this spot the Native Americans lost their grip on the fertile Midwestern lands they had roamed for thousands of years," according to interpreters at the Tippecanoe Battlefield National Historic Landmark.

Tecumseh and his brother, Tenskwatawa, are familiar figures in Indiana history—Shawnees who tried to unite fifty tribes into a coalition to oppose the U.S. government. Their base of operation was Prophetstown along the Wabash River, so named in honor of the younger brother's role as a prophet or spiritual leader of his people.

Tecumseh was not present for the showdown. He was in the South recruiting other tribal nations to join his confederacy.

Harrison was aware of Tecumseh's absence when he marched one thousand troops north from the territorial capital of Vincennes. His army set up camp where the Wabash River meets Tippecanoe Creek, about a mile west of the Indian settlement.

Most histories say Tenskwatawa was directed in a vision to conduct a sneak attack on Harrison's camp, ignoring his brother's warnings to avoid hostilities until his return. A more recent account suggests U.S. sentinels accidentally engaged warriors on night patrol. Regardless of who fired first, full-scale fighting broke out around the encampment.

By sunup, U.S. forces claimed victory. The Indians "quit the battle and melted away into nothingness," said historian Richard J. Reid. Harrison lost thirty-seven men; Native American casualties were not recorded but deemed comparable.

Although the battle lasted a mere two hours, it had been brewing for two decades.

In 1795, after a decisive U.S. victory over Native Americans at the Battle of Fallen Timbers, Tecumseh refused to sign a treaty he considered outright theft of Indian lands in the Ohio region. The treaty

Tippecanoe Battlefield Park is a national historic landmark that features an eighty-five-foot marble obelisk memorializing the battle and General William Henry Harrison.

opened up the Midwest to a flood of settlers and relegated Native Americans to a shrinking corridor of land north of the Ohio River.

In 1808 Tecumseh and his brother moved their headquarters from Ohio to Tippecanoe County (Keth-Tip-Pe-Can-Nunk) at the invitation of the Delaware and Potawatomi tribes living there.

The State Park at Prophetstown is working to restore native habitats, including prairie, wetlands and open woodlands to resemble the nineteenth-century landscape that Native Americans would have experienced.

In 1809 Harrison, governor of the Indiana Territory, negotiated the Treaty of Fort Wayne that purchased 3 million acres from Delaware, Shawnee, Potawatomi, and other tribes. This infuriated Tecumseh, who took a delegation of warriors to Vincennes in 1810 to meet with Harrison and demand that the treaty be rescinded. He argued that the self-appointed chiefs who signed the treaty did not have the right to act on behalf of all, and he urged Native Americans not to give up any more land. That meeting, and another in 1811, convinced Harrison of the threat posed by Tecumseh.

Tippecanoe became known as the opening salvo in the War of 1812, which pitted Great Britain against the infant United States. Tecumseh and most Native American groups fought with the British.

Harrison and Tecumseh met again in that war. On October 5, 1813, Harrison led U.S. troops against British and Native American fighters along the Thames River in Ontario, Canada. Tecumseh was killed on the battlefield—his vision of an effective Indian resistance movement dying with him.

Directions to Tippecanoe Battlefield: Take I-65 to exit 178 (Indiana 43) and follow the signs.

Directions to Prophetstown State Park: Take I-65 to exit 178 (Indiana 43) and follow the signs. GPS address is 5545 Swisher Road, West Lafayette, IN.

FRONTIER VIOLENCE ERUPTED AT PIGEON ROOST

On September 3, 1812, a Native American war party killed more than twenty settlers living in a wooded outpost near present-day Scottsburg, Indiana. Motivated by bounties offered by the British, the perpetrators scalped women and children, torched their log cabins, and left the village in ashes.

The massacre at Pigeon Roost is the most notorious example of frontier violence in Indiana history. To this day, it is shrouded in mystery. As the Indiana Historical Bureau noted, "There are many accounts of this tragedy in which the actions and specific numbers killed vary." This much is clear: The massacre left settlers on guard as the War of 1812 raged in their own backyard.

The United States had declared war on Great Britain in June 1812 in response to British harassment of American ships, occupation of forts, and alleged incitement of Native Americans in the Old Northwest, including Indiana. Indians generally sided with the British, and were encouraged after the fall of Detroit to conduct raids on pioneer settlements throughout the Midwest.

Pigeon Roost was one such place, named after passenger pigeons that used the area as a roosting site, fertilizing the soil and providing a plentiful poultry supply. The village was founded in 1809 by Revolutionary War soldier William E. Collings, who had moved north from Kentucky with family and friends.

Early histories of the episode seem culturally biased, if not inflammatory, by modern sensibilities. Lizzie Coleman's 1904 *History of the Pigeon Roost Massacre* referred to "bands of savage redskins." George Cottman's 1915 *Centennial History and Handbook of Indiana* described the massacre as "the most diabolical event in our Indian history."

Some believe Pigeon Roost was a random but easy target because most men were away in the military service of General William Henry Harrison. This left the remaining residents vulnerable to attack. Some say Pigeon Roost was specifically chosen by the war party of mostly Shawnees.

A 1909 *History of Clark County, Indiana* by Lewis Baird claimed bad blood existed between the Collings family and local Indians because "the Collins [sic] boys had stolen a fawn from the Indians and refused to give it up." The elder Collings was home at the time of the massacre and provided the only armed resistance to the Native Americans, killing at least two of them.

In 1888 the Indiana Historical Society published an account of the incident by Judge Isaac Naylor, a member of the Indiana Territory militia, who had arrived at the site the following day. "Oh, what a mournful scene of desolation, carnage and death met our vision as we beheld the smoking ruins of log cabins and the mangled bodies of men and women and children," Naylor wrote.

Following the massacre, settlers in the areas of Clark, Scott, Jefferson, Harrison, and Knox Counties lived in a state of fear until the Treaty of Ghent ended the war with England on December 24, 1814. For frontier men and women, the treaty symbolized the defeat of the Indians and the barrier they posed to westward expansion.

A monument commemorating the victims was dedicated in 1904 and became a state historic site in 1929.

Directions to Pigeon Roost State Historic Site: From I-65, take exit 29A toward Scottsburg and go east to US 31. Drive south to approximately five miles south of Scottsburg.

A fifty-four-foot-tall monument of Bedford limestone marks the spot of the Pigeon Roost settlement attacked by Native Americans in September 1812.

HARMONISTS SOUGHT TO CREATE A PERFECT SOCIETY

For one shining moment in the early nineteenth century, a group called the Harmonists achieved utopia on the Wabash River. Two hundred years later, their experiment continues to inspire visitors to New Harmony, Indiana.

Founded in 1814 by eight hundred German Pietists and carefully ordered by their leader, George Rapp, the town of New Harmony was an exercise in both religious freedom and economic innovation.

Residents believed they were God's chosen people and devoted themselves to preparation for the Second Coming of Jesus Christ. They renounced private property and practiced celibacy.

Unlike other millennialists, who abandoned worldly activities and took to the rooftops to wait for Jesus, the Rappites felt called to create a good and just society on earth. "That is still the lesson of New Harmony," said Connie A. Weinzapfel, director of Historic New Harmony. "How do people come together for the success of the town where they live?"

By modern standards, the Harmonists were successful indeed. In the course of a decade, they built more than 180 log, frame, and brick structures, including community centers, a granary, a tavern, and a church. At its peak the Harmonie Society had close to nine hundred members.

The Harmonists grew crops and raised merino sheep, planted vineyards and orchards, established a library and school, and started businesses that made pottery, shoes, cloth, and rope. "Their economy was balanced and nearly self-sufficient, and it was very profitable," wrote historian James H. Madison in *The Indiana Way*.

The architecture was especially notable at a time when 70 percent of their frontier neighbors lived in one-room log cabins. A typical Harmonist family dwelling was a two-story frame and brick home modeled after the traditional German hall-kitchen design known as *flurkuchenhaus*.

Rapp and his followers immigrated to the United States in 1803 after being persecuted in Germany for their pietist and pacifist views. The group initially settled in Pennsylvania, but they outgrew that

New and old come together in New Harmony, where the David Lenz House, built by the Harmonie Society, circa 1820, contrasts with the Atheneum visitors center built in 1979.

property and wanted better shipping access, so they moved west and acquired 20,000 acres on the Wabash River in what was still the Indiana Territory.

Citing scriptural reasons, Rapp decided to move the community back east to the Pittsburg area in 1824. He sold the town for $135,000 to Robert Owen, a wealthy industrialist of Welsh descent, and William Maclure, a Scottish philanthropist. The two men sought a ready-made location to launch their own utopian experiment—this one secular and socialist. It lasted only two years, likely because there was little incentive for people to work and no religious commitment to bind them together.

Owen's children remained in Indiana and helped create a culturally and scientifically vibrant community that thrived until the 1850s. Many years later the wife of Owen descendant Kenneth Dale Owen, the late Jane Blaffer Owen, was influential in restoring landmarks from both utopian experiments.

Today New Harmony is a living museum town featuring more than a dozen historic sites and a modern visitors center designed by internationally acclaimed architect Richard Meier.

Directions: Historic New Harmony is thirty miles west of Evansville. From I-64, take Exit 4 and Follow Indiana 69 South seven miles to Indiana 66 West. Indiana 66 leads directly to New Harmony.

INDIANA YEARS SHAPED ABRAHAM LINCOLN

Three states claim Abraham Lincoln as a favorite son, but only Indiana can take credit for his formative years. As he moved through adolescence to adulthood, Lincoln worked, studied, and dealt with adversity on the Indiana frontier.

During this period, Lincoln handled an ax "almost constantly," as he recalled. He also read voraciously and practiced carpentry, even helping his father build a coffin for his mother. Lincoln took a ferry to New Orleans on business and witnessed a slave auction that troubled his soul. He listened and learned from political debates at the local general store.

"Many of the character traits and moral values that made Abraham one of the world's most respected leaders were formed and nurtured here," according to National Park Service historians at the Lincoln Boyhood Home Memorial.

The site is Indiana's most significant tribute to the sixteenth president, preserving some of the original acreage where Lincoln lived from age seven to twenty-one. A working pioneer homestead re-creates what life might have been like for the Lincolns with log cabin, outbuildings, split-rail fences, livestock, gardens, and crops. A Memorial Court features five sculpted panels marking significant phases in Lincoln's life, including his Indiana years.

Those began in late 1816, just as Indiana became a state, when Thomas and Nancy Lincoln moved with their son and daughter from Kentucky to Spencer County, Indiana, then still a forested wilderness. The Lincolns built the first of several cabins on a knoll in the midst of a 160-acre claim near Little Pigeon Creek, and Abe and his father set about clearing land to ready it for planting. "It was a wild region, with many bears and other wild animals still in the woods," Lincoln wrote.

The family has been in Indiana two years when Lincoln's mother contracted a fatal case of milk sickness. The illness is caused by drinking milk or eating meat from a cow that has ingested a toxic plant called white snakeroot.

In 1819 Thomas traveled to Kentucky and married a widow, Sarah Bush Johnston, and the two returned to Indiana with her three children in tow. She also brought a small library, including *Aesop's Fables*,

A re-created 1820s homestead occupies four of the original 160 acres owned by Thomas Lincoln.

Robinson Crusoe, Pilgrim's Progress and *Sinbad the Sailor*. Those stories inspired Lincoln, as did Parson Weems's *The Life of Washington* and Benjamin Franklin's autobiography, which demonstrated the sacrifices the founding fathers had made to create the United States.

Lincoln received only a year or two of formal schooling. His stepmother encouraged him in his attempts to better himself, which he did by studying books and practicing oratory.

In 1830 Thomas moved his family again, this time to Illinois in pursuit of more productive farmland. Abe struck out on his own, settling first in New Salem and later Springfield, where he enjoyed a successful law practice. In 1834 he launched a political career that took him from the Illinois legislature to the White House.

A strong work ethic, a love of learning, a clear sense of right and wrong, a gift for gab, and the intellect to back it up—Lincoln's formative years prepared him well for the Civil War that consumed his presidency.

Directions to Lincoln Boyhood National Memorial: Site is forty-three miles east of Evansville. From I-64, take Exit 57A. Go south on US 231 to the Santa Claus/ Gentryville exit. Turn west on Indiana 162; go two and a half miles to the park entrance on the right.

INDIANA'S FRAMERS MET UNDER FAMOUS ELM TREE

James Madison, Benjamin Franklin, and their colleagues spent almost four months debating, writing, and editing the document that became the U.S. Constitution. It took James Brownlee, Benjamin Parke, and their associates only eighteen days to write Indiana's governing document.

The framing of our first constitution represented the final step in a lengthy and sometimes controversial process that advanced Indiana from frontier territory to full-fledged state.

Territorial leaders had hoped Indiana would be admitted to the Union earlier, following a process laid out in the Northwest Ordinance of 1787, but financial difficulties and the War of 1812 intervened. By 1816 Indiana was back at bat.

Congress passed an enabling act on April 19, 1816, providing for a May election of delegates to a state constitutional convention. The representatives were to meet the next month in the territorial capital of Corydon. They gathered on June 10, 1816. "As a group they were men of high quality," according to an account by the Indiana Historical Bureau.

Patrick Henry Shields was one of them. Educated at Hampton-Sydney College and the William and Mary law school in Virginia, Shields moved to Indiana around 1804 and served as a judge. He was a private under William Henry Harrison at the Battle of Tippecanoe.

John Boone of Harrison County was Daniel Boone's cousin. Jeremiah Cox of Wayne County was a blacksmith. William Eads of Franklin County was a banker and postmaster.

Two future governors were selected to lead the convention: Jonathan Jennings as president and William Hendricks as secretary.

Historian John Dillon said the delegates were "clear-minded, unpretending men of common sense, whose patriotism was unquestionable and whose morals were fair."

Their first task, as required by the enabling act, was to determine whether to proceed immediately toward statehood. On June 11, after considerable discussion, the delegates voted 34–8 for Ezra Ferris's resolution declaring it "expedient, at this time, to proceed to form a Constitution and State Government."

Unlike the Philadelphia delegates, who parsed every clause of the U.S. Constitution, the Corydon convention worked quickly. Most of Indiana's constitution was copied from the constitutions of Ohio, Kentucky, Virginia, and Pennsylvania.

The convention cost taxpayers $3,076, with $200 spent on printing and stitching the constitution and journals, $41.50 on books and stationery, and $27.50 for tables and benches.

When they were not sitting on benches, the delegates could be found under an elm tree. Construction of the state capitol building was not quite finished and the log cabin that served as territorial headquarters was miserably hot, so the delegates took their discussions outdoors. The tree, with leafy branches spanning 130 feet, was dubbed the Constitution Elm and became a symbol of Indiana's founding.

In 1925, despite efforts to save it, the tree died from Dutch elm disease. The branches were cut into souvenirs. The trunk was coated in black creosote and preserved inside a sandstone monument.

Jo Ann Schoen, a lifelong Corydon resident and Patrick Shields descendant, owns two items made from the tree, one of them a paperweight. "When I have guests in town, we always have to go by the elm," Schoen said. "You can't drive anywhere in Harrison County without seeing history."

Directions to Constitution Elm: From North Capitol Avenue in Corydon, go east two blocks on High Street and the elm is on your right.

OPPOSITE: *The dead trunk of the Constitution Elm is on display in a sandstone monument on High Street in Corydon.*

INDIANA BECAME NINETEENTH STATE UNDER MADISON

It is a date every Hoosier should know: December 11, 1816. On that day, Indiana became the nineteenth state.

We have been observing it formally since 1925, when the Indiana General Assembly passed a law requiring the governor to "issue a proclamation annually designating the eleventh day of December as Indiana Day." Indiana Code 1-1-10-1 encourages public schools and citizens to celebrate "in appropriate and patriotic observance of the anniversary of the admission of the state of Indiana into the Union."

Statehood was the culmination of a lengthy process, set out in the Northwest Ordinance of 1787, through which territories proved they had enough population (60,000 "free white inhabitants") and enough political experience to govern themselves.

Among the final steps: Petitioning Congress for statehood, passage of an enabling act by Congress, drafting of a state constitution in June 1816, and August 5 elections of state and local officials and U.S. representative.

"A spirited campaign for the governorship was waged between Jonathan Jennings and Thomas Posey," noted historians John Barnhart and Dorothy Riker in *The History of Indiana*. Jennings won by a vote of 5,211 to 3,934 and took office on November 7. He served two terms, and was later elected to Congress.

Voters elected twenty-nine representatives and ten senators to the first general assembly. Most of the winners had political experience as delegates to the constitutional convention or as members of the territorial legislature. Their introductory session began November 4 in the new state capitol in Corydon. The first order of business was to select the men who would serve as secretary of state, auditor, and U.S. senators—positions that would not be chosen by popular vote until the twentieth century.

On December 11 President James Madison signed into law the congressional resolution admitting Indiana to the union "on an equal footing with the original states, in all respects whatever." That day has been considered Indiana's birthday ever since.

The Indiana General Assembly met in November 1816 in the new Federal-style capitol in Corydon.

If the typical Hoosier does little to celebrate this landmark date, our younger citizens make up for our oversight. Indiana history is taught in fourth-grade classrooms, and many students take part in the Statehood Day Essay Contest, which takes place every year in the fall with finalists invited to the Statehouse for a ceremony in the rotunda.

Corydon is an especially popular field-trip destination because its historic buildings tell the story of Indiana's infancy. The original Federal-style capitol still stands on the town square. Its forty-foot-tall walls were made of limestone from local quarries, testament to what would become a significant Indiana industry.

The first state office building was constructed in 1817 and housed the state auditor and treasurer. The state's money allegedly was kept in a vault in the cellar.

"The Old Capitol was originally built as the Harrison County Courthouse so both the county and state used the building for eight years," said Bill Brockman, former historic site manager.

In 1825 the seat of state government moved north to Indianapolis, and the old capitol continued to function as the county courthouse until 1929. It was restored and opened as a state memorial in 1930.

Directions: From I-64 take exit 105 and turn onto Indiana 135 toward Corydon.

JONATHAN JENNINGS' STORY ONE OF TRIUMPH AND TRAGEDY

In the rough-and-tumble world of frontier politics, Jonathan Jennings experienced the highest of highs and the lowest of lows.

Indiana's first governor, Jennings was credited with pushing Indiana from territory to statehood, defeating an old guard loyal to William Henry Harrison, and insisting that the nineteenth state would not have slavery.

By the time of his death at the young age of fifty, Jennings had suffered political defeat, debt, and health problems caused by years of alcohol abuse. He was buried in an unmarked grave and forgotten by history until the 1893 legislature arranged for a tombstone.

"He was so instrumental in Indiana's statehood," said Bill Brockman, former manager of the Corydon Capitol State Historic Site. Most memorable, noted Brockman, was Jennings's rivalry with Harrison, the Indiana territorial governor and military hero who oversaw much of Indiana's progression toward statehood. The two had different views of what Indiana should become.

"Harrison was generally proslavery and anti-statehood while Jennings was just the opposite," Brockman explained. "Jennings's faction won out and changed the course of Indiana's future."

Ironically, Harrison's popularity as a military hero put him in position to become president of the United States in 1841 (albeit for thirty-one days), while Jennings's alcoholism cost him his career. By 1831 "the once premier Hoosier politician . . . found himself without a public office," wrote his biographer, Randy K. Mills.

Historians consider Jennings Indiana's first professional politician. Although he owned a farm, his income came from government service from the time he moved to Indiana from Pennsylvania in 1806 to his last unsuccessful run for Congress.

While living in Vincennes, Jennings found work as a clerk in a federal land office and strategized career moves. He soon realized options were limited in the Harrison-dominated capital so he moved to Jeffersonville, where more citizens shared his political views.

In his first campaign for territorial delegate to Congress, his supporters attacked the Harrison faction as aristocratic and proslavery.

Jennings died in 1834 and was buried in an unmarked grave. Almost sixty years later, his body was exhumed and moved to Charlestown Cemetery.

The latter was a fair charge due to the territory's Indentured Servant Act, which essentially legalized slavery by permitting contracts with servants that exceeded their life expectancy. The message resonated with voters.

According to Mills, "The 1809 Indiana territorial election for congressional representative featured one of the biggest political upsets in the region's history." Jennings defeated Harrison's choice: Thomas Randolph, "a thirty-eight-year-old Virginian of great refinement." Jennings was twenty-five.

For the next two decades Jennings enjoyed spectacular success. He was reelected territorial delegate in 1811, 1812, and 1814, and he presided over the 1816 convention that drafted the state's first constitution.

Jennings was elected governor in 1816, handily defeating incumbent Territorial Governor Thomas Posey. He was reelected to the governor's office and then spent four terms in the U.S. House of Representatives.

Jennings lost his seat in Congress in 1830 no doubt because he could no longer hide the effects of alcoholism. In Mills's book, the story is told of two passersby who spotted a drunk Jennings leaning against a tree in Charlestown, Indiana. Overhearing one explain that he was a former governor, Jennings said, "Yes, a pretty governor. He can't govern himself."

Jennings died a pauper in 1834 and was buried on his former farm. Almost sixty years later, the Indiana General Assembly appropriated $500 for a modest headstone, and his body was exhumed and moved to Charlestown Cemetery.

Directions: Jennings is buried at Charlestown Cemetery in Clark County. His plot is just north of the cemetery entrance at Pleasant and Harrison Streets.

SLAVERY EXISTED IN FREE INDIANA

Although the Indiana Constitution of 1816 expressly prohibited it, slavery existed in early Indiana. Two court cases filed by enslaved black women helped put an end to the practice.

In the early nineteenth century, Polly Strong and Mary Bateman Clark challenged prevailing attitudes to claim their civil rights as U.S. and Indiana citizens.

"People get really uneasy about saying Indiana practiced slavery," said Eunice Trotter, a Clark descendant who has researched the story. "This is our history and we don't ignore it like it never happened. We embrace it, we learn from it, and we move on."

In a legal sense, slavery was always forbidden in Indiana. The Northwest Ordinance of 1787 prohibited slavery's spread north of the Ohio River into the future states of Ohio, Indiana, Illinois, Michigan, and Wisconsin.

In practice, slavery not only existed but was also accepted by leading citizens. Pioneers moving to Indiana from Virginia or Kentucky, where slavery was legal, considered slaves property and brought them along, sometimes as indentured servants whose contracts exceeded their lifespans. The 1810 census counted 237 slaves and 393 free blacks in the Indiana Territory.

Any questions about their status should have been settled by Indiana's constitution, which declared, "There shall be neither slavery nor involuntary servitude in this state, otherwise than for the punishment of crimes." But it took two lawsuits to enforce the constitutional protection.

After losing her bid for freedom in a Knox County Circuit Court ruling, Clark appealed to the Indiana Supreme Court, which declared her indenture illegal.

Strong had been a slave since birth and became the property of Hyacinth Lasselle of Vincennes around 1808. Lasselle was a tavern keeper and an officer in the Indiana militia. After Indiana became a state, Strong filed for her freedom in Knox County Circuit Court.

Judge Jonathan Doty's ruling reflected the attitudes of many who lived in the former territorial capital: Despite living in a free state, Strong was Lasselle's property because she was born into slavery and had come legally into his possession.

The Indiana Supreme Court in Corydon ordered that Strong be freed, proclaiming: "It is evident that . . . the framers of our constitution intended a total and entire prohibition of slavery in this state; and we can conceive of no form of words in which that intention could have been more clearly expressed."

In 1821 Clark's case came to the state's high court, and again the court minced no words.

Clark was born circa 1801 and purchased in Kentucky by B. J. Harrison, who took her to Vincennes in 1815. There Harrison freed Clark from slavery and signed her to an indenture lasting thirty years.

In 1816 Harrison's uncle, G. W. Johnston, purchased Clark's indenture for $350 and employed her as his housemaid. Johnston had served in the Territorial House of Representatives and as territorial attorney general.

In 1821 Clark asked the Knox Circuit Court to cancel her indenture because she had been forced to serve it. Johnston, however, claimed that Clark had signed the contract of her "own free will."

Although the trial court sided with Johnston, the Indiana Supreme Court found that Clark's service was involuntary and in violation of the 1816 constitution.

The ruling set important precedents. Others who served as indentured servants were freed after filing suits in Knox County. Nationally, the case was a turning point that led to a new understanding of indentured servitude as a form of slavery.

Directions: To see Mary Clark's historical marker, go to the Knox County Courthouse, 111 North Seventh Street, Vincennes.

COMMITTEE PICKED INDIANAPOLIS
AS CAPITAL

Anyone who has ever served on a committee can relate to the old laugh line: A committee is a group of people who keep minutes and waste hours.

Such was not the case in 1820 when ten Hoosier men were named to a committee to find a new state capital. They were focused, efficient, and prescient. Traveling from different counties in southern Indiana, they met at the home of William Conner on the west fork of White River near present-day Noblesville. From there they headed out to scour the middle section of the state.

A clerk accompanied them to record their proceedings. Each received an allowance: two dollars a day and two dollars for every twenty-five miles traveled.

Their official business resembled a camping trip more than a meeting. In preparation for the task, Joseph Bartholomew of Clark County wrote to John Tipton of Harrison County: "You inform me you are preparing a tent to carry on our route to White River. That is very well and in order that I may not be entirely dependent, I will carry the coffee kettle. . . As for the cooking I know you was formerly a very good cook and if you have forgotten I can learn you."

From May 22 to June 7 the committee surveyed land options before settling on an area "at the mouth of Fall Creek . . . 83 miles from Madison, 108 miles from Corydon, 107 miles from Vincennes and 71 miles from Terre Haute." The group intentionally located the new city at the confluence of Fall Creek and White River to maximize access to water for industrial development. Within a year, the area they described would be dubbed Indianapolis.

At the time, the capital was in Corydon, but from the earliest days of statehood Indiana's framers expected to move it north as settlers headed that way, populating former Native American lands. The state constitution set Corydon as the capital only until 1825. An 1816 Enabling Act granted land for a new capital "on such lands as may hereafter be acquired by the United States from the Indian tribes within the said territory."

In October 1818 U.S. Treaty Commissioners Jonathan Jennings, Lewis Cass, and Benjamin Parke met in Saint Marys, Ohio, with

The 1820 committee that chose the site for Indianapolis would not recognize the view enjoyed today by walkers and bikers on the White River Wapahani Trail just north of the confluence of Fall Creek and White River.

Delaware and Miami tribal leaders and negotiated the New Purchase Treaty. The tribes gave up their claims on the middle third of Indiana in exchange for promises of annuities, other economic assistance, and bushels of salt. The treaty cleared the way for the Indiana General Assembly to go capital hunting.

On November 29, 1820, the committee delivered its final report to lawmakers: "In discharging their duty to the state, the undersigned have endeavored to connect with an eligible site the advantages of a navigable stream and fertility of soil while they have not been unmindful of the geographical situation of the various portions of the state to its political center, as it regards both the present and future interests of its citizens." On Janurary 6, 1821, the legislature approved the state's new political center.

The next task was to pick a name for this seat of Indiana government. Although Indianapolis seems obvious now ("polis" means city), it was not without controversy. An article in the January 13, 1821, *Indiana Centinel* mocked the choice, saying, "Such a name, kind readers, you would never find from Dan to Beersheba; nor in all the libraries, museums and patent offices in the world."

Needless to say, the name stuck.

Directions: The White River Wapahani Trail starts at Riverside Regional Park, 2420 East Riverside Drive, Indianapolis, and follows the White River south to White River State Park.

MASSACRE AT FALL CREEK TESTED FRONTIER JUSTICE

In 1975 Jessamyn West wrote a novel based on a true yet astonishing Indiana story. *The Massacre at Fall Creek* recounted the 1824 murders of nine Indians in Madison County and the ensuing trial and death sentences of the white male perpetrators. In the last chapter, a respected white preacher by the name of Caleb turned to his Native American acquaintances to reflect on the executions they witnessed: "This will be remembered as a great day both for the red man and the white man. On this day for the first time white men punished their own kind for killing Indians. . . . Now we will live peacefully together."

Caleb's prediction, like West's book, was fiction. The executions at Fall Creek were not long remembered nor did the case lead to lasting peace. It was a fleeting moment of frontier justice that received scant attention from legal scholars and historians.

Yet this is a story all Hoosiers should know because it reflected pioneer Indiana at its most enlightened.

On the morning of March 22, 1824, a roving band of white men killed a peaceful clan of Seneca and Miami camped along Deer Lick Creek, a tributary of Fall Creek near Pendleton, Indiana.

Three of the victims were women and four were children. One of the men was a subordinate chief of the Seneca, "a person of great distinction and greatly esteemed among the Senecas," according to Conner Prairie historians.

The murderers presumed they could get away with their crime, a reasonable expectation taking into consideration the cultural norms of the day.

Instead, they were hunted down by the citizens of Madison County. Although one suspect escaped, the others—James Hudson, Andrew Sawyer, John T. Bridge, and his son, John Bridge—were charged, tried, convicted, and given the death penalty. "It was perhaps," noted Indiana historian James H. Madison, "the first time in the history of the United States that the law worked with full recognition of Indian humanity."

In his sentencing statement at the conclusion of Hudson's trial, Judge William Wick expressed his outrage. "O my God! How could you

A stone marker bluntly states what happened at this spot along the banks of Fall Creek.

do it?" he asked Hudson. "Did you persuade yourself that because he was an Indian it would be less criminal to take away his life than that of a white man?"

Hudson's hanging took place on January 12; the others on June 3, 1825. A huge crowd including Indian chiefs in full dress gathered around the falls at Fall Creek to watch. In a moment of high drama, Indiana governor James Brown Ray came riding to the scene on horseback to pardon the youngest, eighteen-year-old John Bridge, due to his youth and ignorance.

Although justice had been served, the case set no enduring precedent, and, in coming decades, prejudice toward native peoples hardened. By the middle of the nineteenth century the proverbial stereotype, "the only good Indian is a dead Indian," became the accepted attitude. It would be another one hundred years before federal law recognized Native Americans as having full rights of U.S. citizens.

A stone marker in Falls Park in Pendleton marks the spot of the executions. A state historical marker stands at the massacre site near Markleville. They are enduring symbols of a case that for one shining moment challenged and overcame prejudice on the Hoosier frontier.

Directions: Falls Park is at 299 Falls Park Drive in Pendleton, Indiana.

MARQUIS DE LAFAYETTE A BIG HIT IN JEFFERSONVILLE

A half-century after the Declaration of Independence was issued, the Frenchman who helped the United States win the American Revolution returned to this country on a victory tour. It was a landmark event for cities on his itinerary, including Jeffersonville, Indiana.

The 1824–25 visit to the United States by the sixty-seven-year-old Marquis de Lafayette, last surviving general of the Revolutionary War, dominated headlines for a year. The closest modern equivalent would be a visit from the Pope.

Congress had voted to invite the aging war hero to the United States to thank him for his service to the Continental Army and to reinvigorate republican spirit as a new generation of political leaders moved into power. President James Monroe sent the official invitation. Cities and states that desired his presence passed special legislation.

In January 1825 the Indiana General Assembly adopted a resolution urging Lafayette "to visit this state, at the seat of Government, or such town on the Ohio River as the general may designate."

Accompanied by his son, George Washington Lafayette, the marquis arrived in the United States in August 1824. He spent the fall and winter touring New England, Philadelphia, and Baltimore, with an extended stay in Washington, D.C.

In spring he went south to New Orleans. He then headed north to Saint Louis before traveling east on a route that passed through Nashville, Louisville, Cincinnati, Pittsburgh, Buffalo, and many small towns along the way.

Lafayette took a day trip to Indiana while in Louisville, crossing the Ohio River on May 11 to Jeffersonville, where he was "greeted on the Indiana shore by a salute of thrice 24 guns, discharged from three pieces of artillery stationed on the river bank," according to *Baird's History of Clark County, Indiana* (1909).

Military officers escorted Lafayette to a mansion overlooking the river—the home of the late Indiana Territory governor Thomas Posey. Governor James B. Ray and Revolutionary War veterans were there to meet him. Lafayette attended a public reception followed by a 3:00 p.m.

Lafayette's visit to the United States in 1824–25 inspired the naming of Lafayette, Indiana. The general holds a sword next to his heart in this marble sculpture designed by Lorado Taft for the Tippecanoe County Courthouse in 1887.

dinner held outside on a 220-foot long table decorated with roses and other flowers.

A banner proclaimed, "Indiana welcomes LaFayette, the Champion of Liberty in Both Hemispheres!"—a reference not only to Lafayette's role helping the colonists, but his subsequent, less successful, effort to bring equality and freedom to his own country during the French Revolution.

After dinner, guests offered toasts to the United States, its friends, the memory of George Washington, and "Major General LaFayette united with Washington in our hearts." Lafayette wished the best to Hoosiers, saying, "May the rapid progress of this young state, a wonder among wonders, more and more evince the blessings of republican freedom." The dinner concluded around 6:00 p.m. and Lafayette was escorted back to Louisville, as told in Baird's history.

Lafayette's visit inspired not only the citizens, but also the naming of a city. Kathy Atwell, executive director of the Tippecanoe County Historical Association, said, "Our understanding is that the founder of Lafayette, William Digby, was a great admirer of the Marquis de Lafayette. Digby founded our city in 1825 when the marquis was doing his hero's tour."

Notably Fayette County was named after Lafayette at its founding in 1818, seven years earlier, an indication of the general's enduring popularity long after his contribution to American independence.

Directions: The Tippecanoe County Courthouse is at 20 North Third Street, Lafayette, Indiana.

INDIANA UNIVERSITY BEGAN
AS A SEMINARY IN 1820

When the first classes were held at Indiana University in 1824, the institution had one professor, ten male students, and no building to call its own. The only subjects offered were Latin and Greek. Today, more than 3,000 professors teach 47,000 students on a campus graced by limestone buildings and woodland paths. Undergraduates choose from more than 150 majors.

And that is just at Bloomington. IU has campuses throughout the state and an operating budget of $3.3 billion. Its founders would surely marvel at the size and scope of the tiny school they launched in the Monroe County wilderness.

In the beginning, it was called the Indiana Seminary, but it was not a religious training ground in the sense that word is used today. In early-nineteenth-century parlance, seminary referred to a place of general learning offering coursework beyond reading, writing, and arithmetic.

The Indiana General Assembly created the Indiana Seminary in 1820, naming six men to serve as its trustees. One of them, David H. Maxwell, wrote in 1821 that it was to be a "humble" school where "the elementary parts of an education can be had."

It did not stay humble. In 1828 the legislature turned the seminary into a college and in 1838 gave it university status. In 1852 an act of the legislature declared IU "the university of the state." After a fire destroyed IU's sciences building in 1883, the school moved to its current location on the east side of Bloomington so it could expand to accommodate more buildings and more students.

Early histories say that was the plan from the beginning—IU was destined to be the state university mentioned in Article 9, Section 2, of the 1816 state constitution: "It shall be the duty of the General Assembly . . . to provide, by law, for a general system of education, ascending in a regular gradation, from township schools to a state university, wherein tuition shall be gratis, and equally open to all." More recent scholarship, however, suggests that turning Indiana Seminary into the flagship university was Maxwell's idea that he strategically pushed through the legislature.

There is good reason to believe the intended site for lawmakers' proposed University of Indiana was not Bloomington, but downtown Indianapolis. That story has been obscured by time, memory, and IU's own telling of its creation story, historian Howard E. McMains noted in a 2010 article in the *Indiana Magazine of History.* Consider that designer Alexander Ralston's 1821 mile-square plan for Indianapolis platted locations for the statehouse, county courthouse, public market, governor's mansion, and a state university. All the elements came to pass except the university. The intended site is today a greenspace called University Park.

Although IU today is internationally known, it experienced lean times along the way. McMains wrote that "A lawsuit in the 1850s nearly ended the institution," and the "Civil War reduced enrollment to a mere handful of students." As late as the 1920s, McMains noted, there was talk of moving the institution to the state capital.

Herman B Wells, IU's acclaimed president from 1938 to 1962, is credited with transforming the university into one of the country's top research and professional training institutions.

Although IU is Indiana's oldest four-year university, it is not the state's oldest school of higher learning. Vincennes University gets that title, established under an 1800 Act of Congress organizing the Indiana Territory.

Directions: To see the Sample Gates use the address for Franklin Hall, the building just to the north. It is 107 South Indiana Avenue, Bloomington, Indiana.

The Sample Gates are perhaps the most familiar symbol of Indiana University, serving as the main entrance to the historic section of campus known as Old Crescent.

FREE BLACKS MIGRATED TO INDIANA FROM THE SOUTH

Like other pioneers, they came to Indiana in search of land and liberty and, for the most part, found both. Beginning in the 1820s and continuing until the eve of the Civil War, free African Americans migrated in family groups to Indiana and established farming societies that valued hard work, education, and faith.

More than a dozen such communities were formed before 1860. Greenville Settlement, founded in 1822 in Randolph County, may have been the first. Others developed in Grant, Rush, Gibson, and Vigo Counties. One of the most prominent was Roberts Settlement in Hamilton County. Although most of its residents shared the Roberts surname, the Waldens, Winburns, Gilliams, and others came too.

Their journey began in two slave states, North Carolina and Virginia, where the families lived as free people of color before the Revolutionary War. Most were a mix of African, Native American, and English descent, and "it appears that the African element came from the earliest generation of slavery," according to historian Stephen A. Vincent.

By the early nineteenth century, their freedom was uncertain. Three slave revolts had occurred within one hundred miles of their homes, including the famous Nat Turner Rebellion that resulted in the deaths of sixty white people. In response, southern states rushed to place restrictions on the rights of free blacks. Some decided to leave the South for the Midwest, where slavery had been prohibited since the Northwest Ordinance of 1787.

The founders of Roberts Settlement spent time in western Ohio and Rush Counties before settling permanently near modern-day Arcadia. In July 1835 Hansel Roberts, Elijah Roberts, and Micajah Walden purchased the first homesteads. Historians believe they intentionally located near neighborly Quakers and Wesleyans, the abolitionist branch of the Methodist Church.

By 1870 the community consisted of three hundred people on two thousand acres of productive farmland that included a school and a church. "They strongly valued both religion and education," Vincent said.

A country chapel and cemetery are tangible reminders of the once vibrant Roberts Settlement in Hamilton County.

Even in free Indiana, life was difficult. Black pioneers faced the typical hardships of the wilderness as well as prejudice and hostility from white citizens. In 1841 a free black in Hamilton County was abducted and sold into slavery, much like the case of Solomon Northup told in the Oscar-winning film *12 Years a Slave*. In 1851 Indiana's newly drafted constitution prohibited black immigration—language that was not formally removed until 1881.

"Theirs is a story of perseverance," said Bryan Glover of Noblesville, a descendant of Elijah Roberts, who noted that succeeding generations achieved remarkable success as educators, doctors, and ministers.

As job opportunities expanded in the early 1900s and urban life beckoned, family members dispersed, but their sense of purpose remained. "In essence they were able to leverage the advantages of their Roberts Settlement upbringings as they moved to towns and cities," wrote Vincent, "much as their parents and grandparents had leveraged theirs in the migration from North Carolina to the western frontier."

Today only the church and pioneer cemetery remain, preserved through private donations from descendants. A family reunion has been held there annually since 1925 on the Fourth of July, and plans are in the works to share more widely the settlement's story and artifacts with students of Indiana and African American history.

Directions: Robert Settlement is thirty miles north of Indianapolis, just east of US 31 on 276th Street.

NATIONAL ROAD MOVED PEOPLE, MAIL, AND GOODS

A drive across Indiana on the National Road is a trip back in time. This was the route taken in the nineteenth century by pioneers hauling household goods west in Conestoga wagons, by stagecoaches carrying mail, and by farmers moving crops to markets.

Today it is paved and known as Highway 40. Though it looks nothing like the primitive roadway it replaced, relics are everywhere. In Centerville two original mile markers still stand. In Cambridge City tourists can visit the Huddleston Farmhouse that served as a rest stop for weary travelers. In Stilesville unmarked graves remember twelve travelers who died of food poisoning en route from Ohio to the California gold fields.

The National Road is called "the road that built the nation," and in many ways it built central Indiana.

"Really the road was designed for economic development at a time that term hadn't been coined yet," said Joe Frost, former community preservation specialist with Indiana Landmarks and executive director of the Indiana National Road Association.

The National Road was the country's first federal highway, authorized by Congress in 1806 and designed to facilitate westward migration. Construction began in Cumberland, Maryland, in 1811.

Laborers wielding axes, hoes, and shovels cleared the path. They cut trees, removed stumps, leveled hills, and broke rocks. They laid surface materials. The most advanced was macadam, a blend of pebbles and crushed stone; more typical were wood planks and packed dirt.

Work on the Indiana section began in 1827 at Richmond and ended 156 miles later at Terre Haute in 1834. The cost was half a million dollars.

As the road moved west, settlers followed, crossing the Allegheny Mountains to settle the rich farmland of the Ohio River valley. Towns popped up along the way; taverns, inns, and stagecoach businesses flourished. Indiana's population more than quadrupled between 1820 and 1840, and many arrived via the National Road.

The prosperity was short-lived. By the late 1830s, Congress faced money problems, and the project was suspended as the road reached

The 1841 Huddleston Farmhouse, now a museum operated by Indiana Landmarks, was a convenient rest stop for folks traveling west on the National Road (below) in the mid-nineteenth century.

Vandalia, Illinois, short of its intended terminus at Saint Louis, Missouri.

The federal government began surrendering ownership of the road to states, which implemented toll roads to pay for upkeep within their borders. Indiana was essentially broke and handed operations over to private companies.

Road usage continued to drop as the railroad emerged in the 1850s as the preferred mode of transit. It was not until the invention of the automobile in the early twentieth century that the road was reborn as US 40—this time paved with asphalt, which attracted a new wave of commercial activity. That ended with the development of the interstate system in the 1960s, which again diverted traffic.

Today the road is a tourist destination, recognized as an All-American Road by the Federal Highway Administration because of the two hundred years of history it illustrates.

It is called a "scenic byway," noted Frost, but a more fitting adjective is dynamic. "There are layers of history," he said. "You have pike-towns, row houses, rolling countryside, suburban sprawl."

Indiana Landmarks operates a museum at the Huddleston Farmhouse with exhibitions tracing the history of the road from pioneer times to the present. Tours of the site are offered by appointment by calling (765) 478-3172.

Directions to Huddleston Farmhouse: Take the National Road (US 40) to the west side of Cambridge City.

LIMESTONE: INDIANA'S GIFT TO THE WORLD

It is one of Indiana's best-kept secrets. Limestone quarried from three Indiana counties is responsible for some of America's most impressive structures. It was used to build the Empire State Building, the Pentagon, and the Indiana State Capitol. It bedecks the Biltmore Estate in Asheville, North Carolina; the Tribune Tower in Chicago; and the Greystone Mansion in Beverly Hills.

According to the Indiana Limestone Institute of America, "Indiana limestone projects exist in every American city, in smaller towns and villages, in Canada and in every type of atmosphere."

Here is why: Although limestone is sedimentary rock that can be found anywhere there was an ancient sea, Indiana's is considered some of the best for construction. It is more durable than other types, has a consistent neutral color, and can be cut into large blocks or carved in fine detail.

Its superior quality may have something to do with the way it was pushed and tilted during the great upheaval that created the Appalachian Mountains. Whatever the cause, "the stone is remarkable in the uniformity of its texture and in its freedom from impurities and large fossils," stated Joseph Batchelor in a 1944 history of the Indiana limestone industry.

Deposits of Salem Limestone, the official name used by geologists, protrude along a narrow belt from Greencastle to New Albany. Except for long-abandoned quarries at Salem in Washington County and Corydon in Harrison County, commercial production has occurred exclusively in Owen, Monroe, and Lawrence Counties.

The first quarry opened at Stinesville in 1827. Its stone initially was used in the immediate vicinity for bridge foundations, doorsills, and tombstones; the arrival of the railroad in the 1850s guaranteed a national market.

Demand increased in the 1870s after fires in Boston and Chicago destroyed wooden structures and showed the wisdom of building with stone. An estimated fifty-three quarries were in operation as of 1893. Their reputations lured skilled stonecutters and carvers from England, Scotland, and Italy.

The quarries enjoyed a surge in demand in the 1920s thanks to technical advances in quarrying and fabrication and into the 1930s

The epicenter of Indiana limestone country is the Monroe County Court-house, completed in 1908 and built of locally quarried limestone. It is listed on the National Register of Historic Places.

due to federal projects coming out of President Franklin D. Roosevelt's New Deal. In 1928 Indiana mills sold 413,601 cubic yards valued at $17 million. According to Batchelor, there were thirty-three quarries, twenty-two sawmills, and forty-eight cut-stone mills in operation that year, the high point for the industry. When glass, metals, and synthetic building materials became popular later in the century, limestone began to lose market share.

Today, fourteen stone quarries in Monroe and Lawrence Counties produce 118,000 cubic yards of limestone annually and $26 million in revenue. Although the industry is small compared to its heyday, its future is secure because the limestone supply is considered limitless.

Hoosiers interested in learning more can travel the Indiana Limestone Heritage Trail, which features forty different sites in Lawrence and Monroe Counties. There is also a walking tour of Indiana University, home to one of the largest concentrations of Indiana limestone buildings anywhere. Brochures can be downloaded at http://www.visitbloomington.com/limestone/brochures/.

A commercial limestone quarry operates today near Big Creek in Stinesville, Indiana, not far from where Richard Gilbert opened the state's first quarry in 1827.

The neighborhood east of downtown Bloomington called Vinegar Hill demonstrates use of Indiana limestone through several architectural periods, from Greek Revival to art deco. Many of the homes were built by big names in the limestone industry, including master carvers whose decorative skills were reflected in carvings, ornamental panels, and sculptures adorning the facades.

Directions: The Monroe County Courthouse is located at 100 West Kirkwood Avenue, Bloomington, Indiana.

FLEETING CANAL ERA HAD LASTING IMPACT

In 1825 the Erie Canal was completed to great fanfare. Cannon fire, parades, balls, and speeches celebrated the speed and skill with which New Yorkers built "the longest canal in the world," as one eyewitness erroneously called it. (The Grand Canal of China is longer.)

Two years later, Indiana was busy planning its own transportation marvel. In 1827 Congress authorized a half-million-acre land grant to build a canal that would connect Indiana to Lake Erie at Toledo, Ohio, and extend southwest to the mouth of the Tippecanoe River on the Wabash River. Work on the Wabash-Erie Canal began in 1832.

Over the next decade, Hoosier politicians mapped out a thousand miles of canal routes, locks, and reservoirs. In January 1836 Governor Noah Noble signed the Mammoth Internal Improvement Act to fund them, along with turnpikes and railroads.

The law provided for eight major public-works projects, including extension of the Wabash-Erie Canal to Terre Haute, the Whitewater Canal in southeastern Indiana to link the National Road with the Ohio River, and the Central Canal to stretch from Peru through Indianapolis to Evansville. It established a board of commissioners to borrow $10 million over twenty-five years to finance the projects, to be paid back out of rents, tolls, and profits on the routes once they were up and running.

It failed to work out as planned. A serious economic depression hit the country in 1839, and work stopped on most of the projects. By 1841 Indiana was in financial crisis and could not pay interest on its debt.

Creditors cried foul but in the end got back only half the amount due them plus stock in the one canal system with potential to be profitable: the Wabash and Erie, which was already in service. Its route was reworked to reach Evansville in order to finish the Lake Erie-Ohio River connection.

When completed in 1853, the Wabash-Erie Canal stretched 468 miles and surpassed the Erie Canal in length. For a time it did a booming traffic in people, lumber, livestock, and grain, but by the end of the Civil War it was in disrepair; and its business was supplanted by the railroads, which were faster and more efficient. The canal was abandoned in 1874. "It was a very significant canal, but because it was

A patriotic spirit pervades Metamora, where the Ben Franklin III *is docked along Main Street. The boat was built in 1989 to resemble canal boats of the mid-nineteenth century and is pulled by Belgian draft horses.*

built a little bit later than some of the eastern canals it was not nearly as successful economically," said Dan McCain, president of the Wabash and Erie Canal Association.

The association has preserved a three-mile stretch of the canal at Delphi, where it offers boat rides and runs a museum with an extensive exhibition documenting the history of Indiana's canal era and financial collapse.

Whitewater Canal also became fully operational from Hagerstown to Lawrenceburg and Cincinnati, about seventy-six miles total, but was plagued by frequent flooding and abandoned in 1864. A section of the canal is preserved as a state historic site in Metamora, where visitors can ride a horse-drawn canal boat and visit the nation's only surviving covered bridge aqueduct.

Only eight miles of the planned 296-mile Central Canal were completed and operational, a portion of which is used today as an Indianapolis water source. Starting in the Broad Ripple neighborhood, visitors can walk along the crushed-stone towpath.

Visitors to the Wabash and Erie Canal can enjoy a thirty-five-minute float-ing trip on the Delphi, *a canal boat replica.*

The canal era was short-lived but has been described by one histo-rian as an important stage in our agricultural expansion and "economic diversification toward manufacturing and commerce." It had one other enduring impact: As a result of the experience, when lawmakers rewrote the state constitution in 1851 it contained a provision prohib-iting the state from going into debt.

Directions, Wabash and Erie: GPS address of Wabash and Erie Canal Park is 1030 North Washington Street, Delphi, Indiana.

Directions, Whitewater: The Whitewater Canal Historic Site is at 19073 South Main Street, Metamora, Indiana.

OBSCURE PIONEER POET HAD NATIONAL FAME

James Whitcomb Riley was the most acclaimed, but he was not the first Hoosier poet to gain national fame. Sarah T. Bolton deserves that honor. Even today her poem "Paddle Your Own Canoe" is cited and recited though few know anything about its origins.

Her poetry "was known everywhere," and the canoe poem was set to music and translated into a dozen foreign languages, according to historian Jeanette C. Nolan in her book *Hoosier City*. Indiana Historical Society records note that Bolton served as poet laureate of Indiana during the 1840s and 1850s.

Bolton was born Sarah Tittle Barrett in 1814 in Newport, Kentucky, and moved as a toddler with her parents to the Jennings County, Indiana, wilderness. Not liking the isolation, her father sold the farm and took the family to more civilized Madison when she was nine. There she studied Latin and read Virgil and other classics. Her first published poem appeared in the *Madison Banner* in 1826. She was not quite fourteen.

In 1831 Barrett married local newspaperman Nathaniel Bolton, and the two moved to Indianapolis, where they ran a dairy farm and wrote and immersed themselves in public affairs. Although Sarah Bolton had two children and performed all the traditional duties of a housewife, she was a prominent figure in Indiana and was often asked to write poems for public occasions.

Bolton was a feminist seventy years before women gained the right to vote. She lobbied for women's rights when political leaders were rewriting the state constitution in 1850–51. Her husband served as state librarian from 1847 to 1853 and later as clerk of a U.S. Senate committee and diplomat at Geneva, which gave Bolton the chance to travel across Europe, a subject of many of her poems. Nathaniel died in 1858, and Bolton remarried, but she was always publicly known as Sarah T. Bolton.

Modern critics dismiss her work as sentimental and commercial, as noted in a biographical sketch by the Beech Grove Public Library. Yet evidence is overwhelming that she was held in high regard by her contemporaries. When Bowen-Merrill published a collection of her poems in 1892 under the title *Songs of a Life-Time*, it included an intro-

A community park stands on land where poet Sarah Bolton spent her golden years.

duction by Lew Wallace and a poem by Riley, whose writing careers eclipsed Bolton's by the turn of the century.

Although anthologies of Bolton's poetry are no longer in print, she was widely published for her era. During the Civil War her "Union Forever!" poem was credited with rallying the North. "Paddle Your Own Canoe" remains popular today and is often quoted by advocacy groups seeking to deviate from conventional wisdom. Clarke Kahlo, an environmental activist in Indianapolis, explained, "Paddling your own canoe is a great metaphor for life. We all like to have control."

By 1871 Bolton had retired from the spotlight and bought land at Beech Bank southeast of Indianapolis (now Beech Grove), where she lived her golden years in relative quiet. She died in 1893. Although forgotten by Hoosiers, she is memorialized at a community park purchased by Beech Grove in 1930 from the Bolton Estate. The city's Web site noted, "The park reflects the life and beauty that Mrs. Bolton often spoke of in her poetry."

On a recent summer day, dozens of park visitors were enjoying the picnic areas, athletic fields, and other amenities, but when asked none could say who Bolton was or why the park was named after her. Only a hard-to-find historical marker on Sherman Drive near the park's side entrance offered a brief biographical explanation.

Directions: Main entrance to Sarah T. Bolton Park is at 1300 Churchman Avenue, Beech Grove. The park can also be accessed from Seventeenth Avenue and from Main Street at Fifteenth Avenue.

"Paddle Your Own Canoe"
Sarah T. Bolton

Voyager upon life's sea,
To yourself be true,
And where'er your lot may be,
Paddle your own canoe.
Never, though the winds may rave,
Falter nor look back.
But upon the darkest wave
Leave a shining track.

Nobly dare the wildest storm,
Stem the hardest gale;
Brave of heart and strong of arm,
You will never fail.
When the world is cold and dark,
Keep an aim in view,
And toward the beacon mark
Paddle your own canoe.

Every wave that bears you on
To the silent shore,
From its sunny source has gone
To return no more.
Then let not an hour's delay
Cheat you of your due
But while it is called today
Paddle your own canoe.

If your birth denied you wealth,
Lofty state and power,
Honest fame and hardy health
Are a better dower;

But if these will not suffice,
Golden gain pursue;
And, to win the glittering prize,
Paddle your own canoe.

Would you wrest the wreath of fame
From the hand of fate?
Would you write a deathless name
With the good and great?
Would you bless your fellow men?
Heart and soul imbue
With the holy task, and then
Paddle your own canoe.

Would you crush the tyrant wrong,
In the world's free fight?
With a spirit brave and strong,
Battle for the right.
And to break the chains that bind
The many to the few,
To enfranchise slavish mind
Paddle your own canoe.

Nothing great is lightly won,
Nothing won is lost,
Every good deed nobly done,
Will repay the cost.
Leave to Heaven, in humble trust,
All you will to do:
But if you succeed you must
Paddle your own canoe.

POTAWATOMI FORCED FROM INDIANA AT GUNPOINT

On the morning of September 4, 1838, approximately eight hundred Potawatomi were forced at gunpoint from their homes in northern Indiana and sent on foot and horseback to the "Unorganized Territory" of Kansas to begin a new life.

The march became known as the Trail of Death because forty-two Indians died along the way. Hundreds fell ill during the two-month journey across Indiana, Illinois, and Missouri. A few escaped and returned to Indiana. Most settled around a Catholic mission in eastern Kansas called Sugar Creek.

Their story is not as well known as the Trail of Tears, when more than 4,000 of 15,000 Cherokees died on a similar march from Georgia to Oklahoma. But it occurred for the same reason: to make room for pioneer families in search of fertile cropland.

In 1830 President Andrew Jackson had signed the Indian Removal Act, which gave the president power to negotiate treaties by which Indians would give up their lands east of the Mississippi River in exchange for lands in the West. The removals were supposed to be voluntary, but some tribes did not want to go.

In Indiana Chief Menominee of the Twin Lakes region led the resistance. He accused the federal government of using false means to get younger tribal leaders to sign treaties and of plying them with whiskey that clouded their thinking. "I have not signed any of your treaties, and I will not sign any," Menominee declared. The Treaty of Tippecanoe in 1832 sold the lands in Marshall, Kosciusko, Fulton, Cass, and surrounding counties without his approval.

"He didn't want to go west," said Shirley Willard, Fulton County Historian and former longtime president of the Fulton County Historical Society. "Kansas is much different from Indiana. He said, 'I'm not going to go.'"

White settlers complained to Governor David Wallace about the continued Potawatomi presence and asked him to act. In the summer of 1838 he appointed General John Tipton to head a removal effort.

That was the beginning of the end for Native American tribes in Indiana. In late August, Tipton, with about one hundred armed mili-

George Godfrey of Citizen Potawatomi Nation stands at the Trail of Death highway sign north of Rochester.

tia, traveled to Twin Lakes and rounded up all Potawatomi within a thirty-mile radius. Chief Menominee was tied up like a dog and forced to go west with the others.

Benjamin Marie Petit, a priest from France assigned to missionary work in northern Indiana, accompanied the Potawatomi on the 660-mile trek and kept a journal of the experience. He wrote about the hardships they endured "under a burning noonday sun, amidst clouds of dust, marching in line, surrounded by soldiers who were hurrying their steps."

A similar fate awaited the Indiana Miami, most of whom were forced to move west in 1846. "By the end of the pioneer era," wrote Indiana historian James H. Madison, "there were only scattered Indian people in the state, many of mixed ethnicity, many moving farther from their native cultures, many prudently choosing to hide their Native American connections and pass as white."

By the twentieth century Hoosiers began to see Indian removal as a regrettable chapter in state history that unjustly discriminated against Native Americans. In 1909 the state erected a monument to Chief Menominee's memory about a mile south of Twin Lakes.

Since 1976 the Fulton County Historical Society has remembered the Potawatomi removal with a living history festival each September. Every five years descendants of the Potawatomi join historians and others in a caravan to travel the 660 miles from the Chief Menominee monument to the end of the trail at Saint Philippine Duchesne Memorial Park in Kansas. Historical markers and highway signs note key locations along the route.

Directions: Motorists may follow the Trail of Death beginning at the Chief Menominee monument near Twin Lakes, Indiana, and ending in Kansas. To get to the monument from US 31, turn west on County Road 13 and continue for about five miles. Turn north on Peach Road and go about a half mile.

LANIER MADE A MARK IN BANKING, RAILROADS

James F. D. Lanier twice came to the rescue when Indiana desperately needed his help. Without him, state history might have turned out differently.

Lanier was born in 1800 in Beaufort County, North Carolina, and died in 1881 in New York City. During the interlude, he lived in Indiana and made lots of money in law, banking, and railroads.

His parents moved several times before ending up in Indiana in 1817, one year after statehood. His father opened a dry goods store in Madison, a pioneer town of 150 that Lanier described as primitive woodland: "It was wholly without streets or any improvements fitted to make it an attractive or agreeable place." Madison quickly became attractive and agreeable, in no small measure due to Lanier's efforts.

A lawyer by training, Lanier had wide interests that ranged from politics to business. From 1824 to 1827 he worked as a clerk at the Indiana House of Representatives, maintaining its journal of proceedings and earning $3.50 a day. It took him three days on horseback to travel from Madison to the capitol in Indianapolis—a trip that a few decades later would take four hours on railroad tracks he financed.

In 1833 Lanier left his law practice to help run the State Bank of Indiana, which had a central office in Indianapolis and ten branches in leading towns. Lanier held more shares in the bank than anyone and was president of the Madison branch. During the panic of 1837, the nation's first big recession, banks across the country collapsed while the Bank of Indiana paid dividends of 12 to 14 percent.

Ten years later, Indiana government faced financial ruin, unable to pay interest on an $8 million debt acquired to finance canal construction and internal improvements. Lanier traveled to Europe to meet with representatives of the largest investors, among them the Baron N. M. Rothschild of London, and negotiated the transfer of ownership of most Indiana canals to their bondholders in exchange for a 50 percent reduction in bond value. "The result was, that I was enabled to get up nearly all the outstanding bonds, and was in this way instrumental in placing the credit of the State on the firm basis upon which it has ever since rested," Lanier wrote in his 1871 autobiography. "The State immediately entered upon a career of prosperity which has never flagged to the present moment."

The Lanier home was constructed from 1840 to 1844 using all local materials. The brick was made on-site, and the limestone came from a nearby quarry.

Around the same time, Lanier made his mark as a railroad financier. He was instrumental in the success of the Madison and Indianapolis Railroad and in 1851 moved to New York, where he and a business partner, Richard Winslow, opened a bank specializing in railroad securities.

Although he never returned to Indiana, Lanier came quickly to the aid of Governor Oliver P. Morton during the Civil War. Indiana had only $10,000 in its treasury, and Morton had promised President Abraham Lincoln 10,000 troops to help the Union war effort. Morton was reluctant to call the legislature into session for fear Southern sympathizing Democrats would revoke his power to control the militia. Lanier loaned the Indiana government $1 million to equip troops and to pay interest on the state debt. It was all paid back by 1870.

Lanier's legacy is preserved in Madison at the mansion he built along the Ohio River in the early 1840s. The home was designed by architect Francis Costigan and is considered one of the finest Greek-Revival structures in the country. The home is a state historic site and National Historic Landmark and is open daily with guided tours at the top of the hour.

Directions: The Lanier Mansion State Historic Site is located at 601 West First Street, Madison, Indiana.

FRENCH MISSIONARY FOUNDED NOTRE DAME DU LAC

If he could see it now, Father Edward Sorin would surely marvel at what has become of Notre Dame du Lac, Our Lady of the Lake, the Catholic university he founded in 1842.

These days it is called simply Notre Dame, of course, but for Sorin the lake that inspired the name was providential. The spring-fed Saint Mary's Lake provided not only food, water, ice, and marl for making bricks, but inspiration.

Arriving at South Bend with seven Holy Cross brothers on a frigid day in late November, Father Sorin took in the scene and declared it "beautiful."

"The lake, especially, with its broad carpet of dazzling white snow, quite naturally reminded us of the spotless purity of our August Lady whose name it bears, and also of the purity of soul that should mark the new inhabitants of this chosen spot," he wrote in a letter dated December 5, 1842.

Sorin, a missionary from France, had traveled from the Catholic diocese in Vincennes with instructions from the bishop to convert 640 acres in Saint Joseph County into a place of higher learning. The land had been held in trust since being purchased from the U.S. government for a Catholic mission to Native Americans.

The University of Notre Dame was officially chartered by the Indiana General Assembly on January 15, 1844. At first it was a modest venture offering preparatory and grade schools, a manual-labor school, and training for the priesthood, in addition to a small classical college attended annually by a dozen or so students.

After a fire destroyed most of the university in 1879, Sorin vowed to expand the school and its curriculum. He said the fire was a message from above that he had not dreamed big enough. "Tomorrow we will begin again and build it bigger, and when it is built we will put a gold dome on top with a golden statue of the Mother of God so that everyone who comes this way will know to whom we owe whatever great future this place has," he said.

Three hundred workers, toiling from dawn to dusk, completed construction on a new building within four months of Sorin's pronouncement. A golden dome was added in 1882, topped by a nineteen-foot-

Old College, constructed in 1843, is the oldest surviving building on the Notre Dame campus. It houses male students pursuing religious vocations.

tall, 4,000-pound statue of Mary. The Main Building still stands and provides classroom space and offices for administrators.

By the time Sorin died in 1893, Notre Dame was on its way to becoming a premier research university and had launched a football program that became world famous under Coach Knute Rockne in the 1920s. Today, more than 12,100 students attend its four undergraduate colleges, architecture school, law school, and graduate school, and admission is competitive with six applicants for every spot.

Peter Lysy, senior archivist and records manager at Notre Dame, has no doubt Sorin would be pleased with how things turned out—once he overcame his shock at the changed demographics. Formerly an all-male institution, Notre Dame's student body today is almost half women and 23 percent minority.

Drawing 2.15 million visitors a year, Notre Dame is one of the most popular tourist sites in Indiana. "If Father Sorin looked at it objectively," Lysy said, "he would be very happy with the school, the prestige, the academic quality, and the influence Notre Dame has."

Directions: From downtown South Bend, go north on US 31/Indiana 933 to Angela Boulevard. Turn right onto Angela, and then turn left at the second stoplight (Eddy Street). Follow signs to visitor parking.

RILEY REVERED FOR HIS HOMESPUN POETRY

Today his poems are written off as the sentimental musings of a time gone by. During his life, James Whitcomb Riley ranked with Henry Wadsworth Longfellow and Mark Twain as a best-selling author, and his works were required reading in virtually every U.S. school.

Many historians consider Riley our most famous Hoosier, not only for the national acclaim he received but also for the public image he created of Indiana.

"More than any other citizen of Indiana, James Whitcomb Riley has carried the fame of his native state into the schools and homes of the world," declared Governor Samuel Ralston in 1915.

Poetry magazine, the oldest monthly journal devoted to verse in the English-speaking world, said after Riley's death in 1916: "He made the world love his Indiana—his cheerful, whimsical, unassuming, shrewd and sentimental neighbors."

Riley was born on October 7, 1849, in Greenfield, the third of six children of Reuben and Elizabeth Riley. His father was a lawyer and Civil War soldier. His mother was a housewife and part-time poet who enjoyed helping the neighbor children put on skits for their friends.

Riley, a school dropout at age sixteen, did not set out to be a poet, but he had inherited his mother's artistic sensibility. His father wanted him to be a lawyer. Riley wanted to be an actor. "The nearest thing in that line I could do was to give public readings," noted Riley. These were a popular form of entertainment in the nineteenth century, combining lectures, poetry, and musical interludes, and they were a perfect venue for Riley to recite his homespun stories and verse. At first crowds were small, so Riley held odd jobs to make ends meet.

In 1875 Riley received his first check for a published poem and left Greenfield for a circuit-rider's life, writing and reciting poems in any city that invited him. In the 1880s, he was booked for performances almost daily and shared the stage with the likes of Twain and Bill Nye.

Riley was best known for the dialect that characterized his most popular poems, including "Little Orphant Annie" and "The Raggedy Man." More than half of Riley's poetry was written in down-home country speech that endeared him to ordinary folks who considered some poems too highbrow.

James Whitcomb Riley spent his boyhood years at
this house, built by his father in 1850. The home is open to the public April
through October (closed Sundays and major holidays) and by appointment.
INSET: A docent shows off the rafter room mentioned in Riley's "Little
Orphant Annie," a poem that warns children, "The Gobble-uns 'll git you ef
you don't watch out!"

"There was a time in American literature when sales of poetry volumes easily matched those of the novels and nonfiction works constituting today's bestseller lists; a time when farm families after a full day of work would hitch up their teams and drive twenty miles over dirt roads at night to hear a favorite poet perform his or her work; a time when newspaper staffs regularly included poets," literary scholar Paul H. Gray noted. "The heyday of this remarkable social phenomenon lasted almost sixty years from 1870 to 1930." It was the era of Riley.

By the time of his death, Riley had written more than one thousand poems, which can be found in *The Complete Poetical Works of James Whitcomb Riley* published by Indiana University Press.

Poetry lovers can visit several sites connected to Riley that explore his legacy. The City of Greenfield owns and operates Riley's childhood home and museum on Main Street. A life-size Riley sculpture stands on the lawn of the Hancock County Courthouse a few blocks away.

In Indianapolis the James Whitcomb Riley Museum preserves the Lockerbie Street home of Mr. and Mrs. Charles L. Holstein, with whom Riley lived from 1893 until his death. A column-style memorial marks Riley's grave at Crown Hill Cemetery, one of the highest spots in Marion County, offering an impressive view of the city where Riley spent the last years of his life.

Directions: The Riley childhood home and museum are located at 250 West Main Street, Greenfield. The Riley Museum is located at 528 Lockerbie Street, Indianapolis.

COFFINS HELPED FUGITIVE SLAVES ESCAPE TO CANADA

Once runaway slaves made it to the home of Levi and Catharine Coffin in eastern Indiana, they were safe. Truly safe. To the best of Levi's knowledge, every slave who passed through his Underground Railroad station made his or her way to freedom.

The Coffins lived in a mostly Quaker community called Newport, now Fountain City, on the front line of the abolitionist movement. Levi was the "president," his house the Grand Central Station of a network of secret routes and safe houses that moved slaves from bondage in the South to freedom.

"You're standing on the same floor the Coffins stood on, the same floor slaves walked on," Eileen Baker-Wall told visitors to the Levi Coffin State Historic Site. Baker-Wall, a volunteer docent, likes to show tourists a display case containing wooden shoes that belonged to her great-great grandfather, William Bush. He was an escaped slave who ended up staying in Wayne County and working as a blacksmith.

Bush was unusual in that regard. For the vast majority of slaves, Fountain City was a momentary stop en route to Canada. There they

The Coffin home, at the center of a Quaker abolitionist community, was a safe haven for slaves traveling the Underground Railroad. INSET: Docent Eileen Baker-Wall, great-great granddaughter of an escaped slave who made his home in Wayne County, leads visitors on a tour of the Coffin historic site.

would be beyond reach of the Constitution's Fugitive Slave Clause, which required the return of runaway slaves to their state of origin.

The Coffins, like many Quakers, felt called to ignore that particular clause in order to live out their belief that all people were created in God's image. "Both my parents and grandparents were opposed to slavery, and none of either of the families ever owned slaves," Levi wrote in his memoir, "so I claim that I inherited my anti-slavery principles."

The family came to Indiana from North Carolina, a slave state, in 1826. Upon his arrival, Levi opened a merchandise store whose profits subsidized his antislavery activities. "In the winter of 1826–27," he wrote, "fugitives began to come to our house."

It was a prime location for a depot because three routes converged there; slaves typically crossed out of slave territory via the Ohio River at Madison, Jeffersonville, or Cincinnati.

In 1839 the Coffins built a Federal-style brick home ideal for hiding fugitives. Slaves entered through the north door into the dining room, where they would warm up by a fireplace and be served a meal prepared by Catharine. Twin beds in an upstairs bedroom concealed a rafter room large enough to hide a dozen or more people. The house had an underground well in its basement that allowed the family to conceal the amount of water used to care for their guests.

Baker-Wall said there is no evidence the house was ever searched by slave hunters. Levi was versed in law and barred entry to any who lacked requisite legal papers, which took so long to obtain that slaves could be well on their way to the next station by the time the slave hunters returned.

In 1847 the Coffins moved to Cincinnati, where they continued with their abolitionist activities. They opened a free-labor store that boycotted products from southern states and sold only goods produced by wage-earning workers. Coffin died in 1877, twelve years after the Civil War brought slaves the freedom he had fought for.

During their two decades in Indiana, the Coffins helped an estimated two thousand slaves go north. Their home is considered one of the best-documented Underground Railroad sites in the country.

Directions: The Levi Coffin House is at 113 US 27 in Fountain City. It is open to the public seasonally and by special arrangement.

1851 CONSTITUTION HAS KEPT INDIANA DEBT FREE

"To the end that justice be established, public order maintained, and liberty perpetuated; we, the people of the state of Indiana, grateful to Almighty God for the free exercise of the right to choose our own form of government, do ordain this constitution." Preamble, Indiana Constitution

Legal scholars say you can learn much about a society by reading the documents that organize its institutions. Using the Indiana constitution as our yardstick, here is what Hoosiers value: a fair legal system, public education, financial solvency, and liberty, especially freedom of religion and freedom of thought.

These ideals were firmly established in the 1851 constitution that remains the foundation of Indiana government. That constitution, submitted to and approved by voters, replaced the original 1816 document famously written under a Corydon elm tree.

The biggest change from the first to the second constitution? "The prohibition on state debt," said Ralph Gray, retired Indiana University–Purdue University at Indianapolis history professor and author of a dozen books on Hoosier history. "It has kept the state out of financial trouble, and that has really helped us over the years."

Indiana has the eighth oldest constitution in the nation, one of the shortest at 10,230 words and "one of the least modified," according to the Indiana Historical Bureau.

The rewriting occurred as a result of a provision in the 1816 constitution that called for a survey every twelve years to determine if voters favored a constitutional convention. By 1849 those wanting change outnumbered those opposed 81,500 to 57,418.

Delegates gathered in the House of Representatives in Indianapolis on October 7, 1850, to begin the drafting process. Sixty-three were farmers, reflecting the state's agricultural economy, and thirty-seven were lawyers. Others in attendance: eighteen doctors, ten merchants, a millwright, a teacher, and a bricklayer.

Most of their modifications were deemed necessary for more effective governance. For example, the convention replaced annual sessions of the legislature with biennial ones after experience proved there was not much for lawmakers to do each year. Delegates agreed that more offices should be elected by voters rather than appointed by the general assembly. The terms for governor and lieutenant governor were changed from three to four years to correspond to legislative sessions.

The state was prohibited from incurring debt except "to meet casual deficits in the revenue; to pay the interest on the state debt; to repel invasion, suppress insurrection, or, if hostilities be threatened, provide for the public defense." That language was in response to the state's near bankruptcy in the 1840s from overspending on canals and other infrastructure projects.

The delegates gave the Bill of Rights top billing in Article I, echoing many principles first stated in the Declaration of Independence, including "that all people are created equal; that they are endowed by their creator with certain inalienable rights; that among these are life, liberty, and the pursuit of happiness."

"The new constitution was not a perfect document," noted Indiana historian James H. Madison. Most notably, the convention's understanding of equality reflected the prejudices of the day. Delegates debated but rejected efforts to give women property rights. Article 13 prohibited African Americans from migrating to Indiana, despite the fact 11,262 blacks were Hoosier citizens as of the 1850 census. Article 13 was nullified by the U.S. Constitution's Fourteenth Amendment, adopted after the Civil War, which granted blacks citizenship rights and equal protection of the laws. Article 13 was formally removed from the Indiana constitution in 1881.

To its credit, Madison said, the new constitution retained many of the best features of its predecessor "and it continued a basic framework that enabled Indianans to govern themselves largely as they wished."

Directions: Indiana's constitutions are on display in the Statehouse Rotunda when the Indiana General Assembly is in session. The address is 200 West Washington Street, Indianapolis.

OPPOSITE: Tourists examine a display case that holds the restored state constitutions from 1816 and 1851. The case has special environmental and security features to protect the documents.

GEORGE JULIAN SERVED INDIANA AS RADICAL REPUBLICAN

George Washington Julian did not think much of compromise. In the decades before the Civil War, he was Indiana's most radical abolitionist. Although he is little known by Hoosiers today, Julian made a lasting mark on the national scene.

"He was always the ready champion of the principle of fundamental democracy—'equal rights for all, special privileges for none,' regardless of race, color, creed, or sex," Indiana historian James Albert Woodburn wrote of Julian in 1915.

"Six feet tall, broad shouldered, with a bit of a stoop, Julian was impossible to miss, and a trial to his more moderate colleagues, because there was little or no give in him," according to another account.

Julian represented the far end of the abolitionist movement in Indiana. Like the rest of the country before the Civil War, Hoosiers were conflicted about slavery. Indiana was a free state with an active Underground Railroad, but most Hoosiers did not believe in mixing the races. Julian, a white man, championed black equality.

The state's 1851 Constitution had declared, "no negro or mulatto shall come into or settle in the state," language approved by voters by a 5–1 margin. Many prominent Hoosiers belonged to the Indiana Colonization Society, part of a national movement to relocate African Americans to what is today Liberia.

Julian's views were shaped by his Quaker upbringing in Wayne County, the most progressive part of the state on the eve of Civil War. A lawyer by training, Julian practiced in Greenfield and other small towns and served in the Indiana House of Representatives in 1845. He had been elected as a member of the Whig Party, the forerunner of the Republican Party.

In 1848 Julian helped found the Free-Soil Party, a one-issue group dedicated to stopping the spread of slavery in the West. He was elected to Congress that year by a narrow margin after a bitter campaign focused on the future of slavery. Years later he remembered it with anguish: "The friends of a life-time were suddenly turned to enemies, and their words were often dipped in venom." He lost his bid for re-election.

The contribution of George Washington Julian is remembered in the historic Irvington neighborhood on the east side of Indianapolis, where a school (above) is named in his memory. Julian's brick Italianate home at 115 South Audubon Street (top) still stands and is privately owned.

In 1852 Free-Soilers chose Julian as vice presidential running mate with presidential nominee John P. Hale of New Hampshire. The two received 155,210 popular votes but no electoral votes.

Two years later, passage of the controversial Kansas-Nebraska Act in Congress led to the formation of the Republican Party. The law opened up western lands to new settlement and allowed for expansion of slavery with citizens' consent, repealing an 1820 law that barred slavery north of the 36 degree 30 minute latitude line. The law infuriated Abraham Lincoln and Julian, among others, and they became founding members of the Republican Party.

In 1860 voters chose Lincoln for president and sent Julian to Congress, where he served for a decade. There he worked with Radical Republicans Charles Sumner of Massachusetts and Thaddeus Stevens of Pennsylvania in crafting national policy for ending slavery, bringing blacks into the mainstream, and rebuilding the country after the war. Julian also advocated for women's suffrage, but it was an idea before its time.

When his political career ended, Julian settled in Irvington, a cultural enclave on the east side of Indianapolis and original site of Butler University. He wrote articles, practiced law, and hosted political notables, including Benjamin Harrison, Frederick Douglass, and Sojourner Truth. He died in 1899; his memory lives on in Irvington, where a public school is named in his honor.

Directions: The historic Irvington neighborhood is five miles due east of downtown Indianapolis on East Washington Street. The George W. Julian School is at 5435 East Washington Street.

CALEB MILLS: THE FATHER OF INDIANA'S PUBLIC SCHOOLS

Indiana's 1816 Constitution called for a statewide system of free public schools, but it did not happen until the 1850s—after education reformers demanded it.

The chief lobbyist for taxpayer-funded schools was Caleb Mills, who used the power of the pen to persuade lawmakers that illiteracy was a threat to Indiana's future. He has been called the father of the Indiana public school system ever since.

Born in New Hampshire in 1806 and educated at Dartmouth College, Mills came to Indiana in 1833 as the first faculty member of Wabash College in Crawfordsville. He was one of many reform-minded educators frustrated that Indiana's constitution gave only lip service to the goal of free education for its children.

To the extent schools existed in Indiana at that time, they were locally operated, poorly funded, charged tuition, and were open only a few months a year—not what the 1816 constitution had envisioned.

Starting in 1846 Mills wrote policy briefs to the Indiana State Senate and House of Representatives urging statewide organization and funding of schools. He signed his missives with a pseudonym, "One of the People," disclosing his real name only before writing his sixth and final message. "They are the most important documents ever prepared on the subject of education in Indiana," according to Indiana historian James H. Madison.

Mills used statistics from the 1840 U.S. Census to make his point: One in seven adults could not read or write, an illiteracy rate that exceeded that of all other northern states and three slave states. His proposed solution was a statewide tax and a centralized school system under a superintendent of public instruction.

The Indiana General Assembly responded by calling a special convention to consider the issue in 1847. Prominent reformers attended, including Ovid Butler, founder of what became Butler University; Presbyterian pastor and abolitionist Henry Ward Beecher; and Calvin Fletcher, a state senator with interests in farming, banking, and railroads.

Caleb Mills built this home in 1836 and lived there for forty-three years. Today Wabash College operates it as a meeting site and guesthouse for campus visitors.

A committee appointed by the Common School Convention reported back that only 37 percent of 129,500 school-age children attended common schools and that "those who attend school at all generally do it for only a small part of the year."

Lawmakers made modest attempts to improve the situation over the next few years, and when the state constitution was rewritten in 1850–51 the education language—deemed visionary, albeit unenforced, in 1816—was further strengthened. It declared:

> Knowledge and learning, generally diffused throughout a community, being essential to the preservation of a free government; it shall be the duty of the General Assembly to encourage, by all suitable means, moral, intellectual, scientific, and agricultural improvement; and to provide, by law, for a general and uniform system of Common Schools, wherein tuition shall be without charge, and equally open to all.

In 1852 the general assembly brought the constitutional language to life by passing the School Law of 1852. This established a common school fund, a centralized system of school organization, and a superintendent of public instruction—all ideas Mills had advocated in his writings. Mills himself served as the state's second superintendent from 1854 to 1857 and then returned to Crawfordsville, where he lived until his death in 1879.

Civil War and adverse rulings from the Indiana Supreme Court slowed the momentum of school reformers for a period, but after the war Indiana's public school system took off. The average length of the school term doubled from sixty-eight days in 1866 to 136 days in 1879. Enrollment grew from 390,714 in 1866 to 511,283 in 1880.

Directions: The Caleb Mills House is adjacent to the Lilly Library on the Wabash College green. From I-74, go four miles into downtown Crawfordsville. Turn south on US 231 and continue three blocks to Wabash Avenue.

DUBLIN HOSTED INDIANA'S FIRST WOMAN'S RIGHTS CONVENTION

Hoosier women have come a long way since the mid-nineteenth century, when a proposal for women's suffrage generated more scorn than acceptance.

One political leader summed up the views of the day when he noted that women already enjoyed "the rights which the Bible designed them to have in this Christian land of ours."

By 1847 married women had obtained limited property rights in Indiana, but the right to vote was still a fanciful idea.

"Few people took it seriously and many ridiculed it or looked upon it as a dangerous manifestation of radicalism, contrary to the teachings of the Scripture," noted historian Emma Lou Thornbrough in her book *Indiana in the Civil War Era.*

In October 1851, three years after Lucretia Mott and Elizabeth Cady Stanton organized a woman's rights convention in Seneca Falls, New York, Indiana suffragists organized a similar meeting at Dublin in Wayne County. They declared that until women demanded "their rights politically, socially and financially, they will continue in the future as in the past, to be classed with negroes, criminals, insane

This marker along the National Road in Dublin marks the spot where early feminists held Indiana's first woman's rights convention.

persons, idiots and infants." While their rhetoric seems indelicate today, it launched a movement that did not quit until the Nineteenth Amendment was added to the U.S. Constitution in 1920.

The Dublin delegates adopted a constitution that called for annual meetings with reports to be given on working conditions and pay, legal rights, and education of women. In 1852 the convention met in Richmond and formally created the Indiana Woman's Rights Association.

In 1859 more than one thousand Hoosiers signed a petition urging the legislature to grant equal political rights to women and to eliminate laws that made distinctions on account of gender. The issue was referred to a committee, which reported back that it saw no need for legislation at that time.

The association was inactive from 1859 to 1867 as the debate about slavery and the Civil War eclipsed the concerns of women. At both state and national levels, efforts to tie women's rights to black rights and abolitionism were unsuccessful.

State efforts picked up steam after the territorial legislature of Wyoming granted women the right to vote in 1869. Colorado, Utah, and Idaho followed suit in the nineteenth century.

In Indiana one feminist forced the issue by attempting to vote in Lafayette in the November 1894 election. After Helen Gougar was turned away by the Tippecanoe County Election Board, she filed a lawsuit alleging her rights had been violated. The case went to the Indiana Supreme Court, where Gougar argued the case herself. The justices denied her arguments, ruling that voting was a privilege not a right, and "it is held only by those to whom it is granted," i.e. men, according to the terms of the 1851 state constitution.

Popular support for women's suffrage grew during World War I due to the significant role women played on the home front. In 1917 the Indiana legislature approved a law allowing women to vote in presidential elections.

In 1920 the Nineteenth Amendment to the U.S. Constitution gave women the vote in all elections. The Indiana constitution was amended the following year to reflect women's new political standing.

Directions: The Woman's Rights Convention historical marker is at 2224 Cumberland Road in Dublin at the corner of US 40 and Davis Street.

T. C. STEELE CELEBRATED THE HOOSIER LANDSCAPE

He was educated in Europe and trained to emulate the brush-strokes of the Great Masters, yet Theodore Clement Steele's greatest gift was in depicting and interpreting the Indiana countryside.

T. C. Steele, Indiana's most famous painter, was born in Gosport in 1847, raised in Waveland, and died at his House of the Singing Winds in rural Brown County in 1926. He loved Indiana, and Indiana still loves him. His paintings sell for upwards of $25,000.

"It boils down to the images," said art dealer Jim Ross of Eckert and Ross Fine Art of Indianapolis. "He painted local subjects and scenes in an agreeable impressionistic style that has wide appeal to Hoosiers."

Steele was the lead character in the Hoosier Group, five acclaimed painters of the late nineteenth and early twentieth centuries who studied abroad to hone their skills and returned to Indiana to paint scenes "en plein air" (in open air). The others were J. Ottis Adams, William Forsyth, Otto Stark, and Richard Gruelle.

The group received its name in 1894 from Chicago art critic Hamlin Garland, who saw their pictures at an exhibition at the Indianapolis Denison Hotel. A month later Chicago hosted the same exhibition, which introduced the artists to a national audience.

The five earned their reputations the old-fashioned way—through study, practice, and hard work. "Because of Steele and the others, Indiana enjoys today one of the top regional art histories in the entire country," Ross noted.

Steele was a student at the Waveland Institute, a preparatory school near Crawfordsville, where he received his first formal instruction in art. By age thirteen he was giving fellow students lessons. By sixteen he was painting portraits; he received his first commissions in 1869.

In his 1870 diary, Steele pledged to dedicate his life to art. He wrote, "The two great qualities that an artist must possess, and that are essentially necessary to all who pass the point of mediocrity, are first an innate and deep love of the beautiful. Secondly, mechanical skill."

T. C. Steele built this studio in 1918 primarily for exhibiting his artwork and entertaining.

His expertise came during five years at the Royal Academy in Munich, an education financed by thirteen Indianapolis art patrons in exchange for "paintings from his own easel as soon as practicable after his return from abroad." When not in the classroom, Steele spent hours in museums copying paintings by Rembrandt, Rubens, and Titian; and visiting art galleries with his wife, Libbie, and their three children.

In 1885 the family returned to Indianapolis, where Steele opened an art school and painted portraits, his primary source of income. His true love was the Indiana countryside and the challenge of capturing light and color of the four seasons.

After his wife's death in 1899, Steele poured himself into his landscapes. He bought 211 wooded acres in Brown County, remarried, and built a pyramid-roofed cottage and studio that overlooked a picturesque valley. It was dubbed the House of the Singing Winds due to breezes blowing through the screened porches. Other artists followed him to Brown County, and an artist's colony developed around Nashville, which continues to this day.

Steele's last home and studio are preserved as a state historic site and guided tours are available year-round. More than fifty of his paintings are on display, and visitors are encouraged to enjoy the site's gardens and hiking trails.

Directions: The T. C. Steele State Historic Site is at 4220 T. C. Steele Road in Nashville.

BOAT PRODUCTION BIG BUSINESS IN NINETEENTH CENTURY—AND TODAY

Drive along the Ohio River in Jeffersonville and you cannot miss the sixty-eight-acre Jeffboat plant, where workers make the ships that transport so much of the nation's grain, coal, and chemicals to market.

Due to our landlocked location, most Hoosiers do not see Indiana as a leader in the shipbuilding economy, yet it is a role the state has been playing for almost two centuries at the same spot where Jeffboat now stands.

"Look out the window and you can see a barge being built," said Lowell Smith, a docent at the Howard Steamboat Museum across the street from the nation's largest inland shipbuilder. "They've been building boats here for a long time."

Indeed, boat builders have occupied the site since 1820, four years after Indiana statehood. Robert C. Green came first, followed by William and Henry French, who sold their shipyard to nineteen-year-old James Howard in 1834. Three generations of Howards operated the yard until the U.S. Navy acquired it in 1941.

The museum preserves memorabilia from the steamboat era—roughly the 1830s through 1900—and is housed in a twenty-two-room Romanesque Revival mansion built by Edmonds Howard and his family in 1894.

In the days before the steamboat, there was no good way to travel or move products. Flatboats carried goods, but going upstream took forever. When a flatboat reached its destination, it was usually taken apart and sold for lumber, and its crew walked or rode horses home.

John Fitch built the first steamboat in America in the 1780s, and Robert Fulton made the invention a success. His boat, *The Clermont*, took the first commercial voyage up the Hudson River from New York City to Albany and back in 1807.

Steamboats were on the Ohio River by 1811, and within thirty years there were hundreds carrying passengers and products down the Mississippi River to New Orleans, an eight-day trip. (Businessmen briefly entertained using the White River, but the idea was abandoned in 1831 after the *Robert Hanna* ran aground upstream of Indianapolis, suggesting the river was not commercially navigable.)

James Howard founded the Howard Shipyards in 1834, and his son built this home across from the Ohio River in 1894.

Jeffersonville, New Albany, and Madison were the most prominent Indiana ports, but steamboats also traveled the Great Lakes. Michigan City became a key port for lake steamboats carrying products east on the Saint Lawrence River to the Atlantic Ocean.

By far the most innovative boats were built by the Howard brothers of Jeffersonville, whose vessels "had an especially fine reputation for speed, comfort and carrying capacity," observed historian Emma Lou Thornbrough in her book *Indiana in the Civil War Era*.

Built in 1878, the *J. M. White* was the Howard brothers' most famous boat. "Few boats could match the technological innovations on board and none could match her speed," according to one account. "The *J. M. White* had chimneys eighty-one feet tall, she had a five tone whistle, and much of the loading machinery she used was steam powered, a significant innovation at the time."

Although inland water transport declined with the advent of the railroad in the 1870s, shipbuilding continued. The navy yard was a major builder of tank landing ships during World War II and now, under ownership of American Commercial Lines, produces towboats and barges.

The three Indiana ports today—Jeffersonville, Mount Vernon and Burns Harbor—contribute $6 billion a year to the state economy. Did you know? More than half of Indiana's border is water, which includes four hundred miles of direct access to the Great Lakes and the Ohio-Mississippi River system.

Directions: The Howard Steamboat Museum is at 1101 East Market Street, Jeffersonville.

WEST BADEN AND FRENCH LICK OFFERED LUXURY IN THE COUNTRY

The infirm frequented French Lick for its miraculous Pluto Water. The rich and famous came to golf—and gamble.

Since the 1830s, the rolling hills and springs around the small town of French Lick have drawn tourists to remote southern Indiana. They still do, thanks to a mammoth restoration of its two historic resorts completed in 2006 and 2007 by the late philanthropist Bill Cook.

"The mineral springs were the original magnet," noted author Chris Bundy in his history of the French Lick Springs and West Baden Springs hotels. Located within a mile of each other, the structures loom large over State Road 56 in Orange County.

Even before Indiana was a state, the area was famous, known as Salt Licks due to abundant mineral licks that attracted bison and, later, pioneers in need of salt for preserving meat. As the story goes, explorer George Rogers Clark renamed the area French Lick because the French were first to settle there. The spring water was valued for

The West Baden Springs Hotel was dubbed the Eighth Wonder of the World due to its massive unsupported dome, reinforced by twenty-four steel girders that fan out from a central hub.

American flags dress up the veranda of the French Lick Springs Hotel.

its sulphates, known to have laxative effects and believed to be good for an array of other ailments, from asthma to malaria.

The first hotel on the French Lick site was built in 1844–45 by Doctor William A. Bowles, who figured out how to bottle the water for sale. He marketed it as Pluto Water after the Greek god of the underworld.

John Lane managed the inn while Bowles served in the Mexican-American War. Upon Bowles' return, Lane set up a competing hotel a mile east. He called it the Mile Lick Inn and labeled his water Sprudel Water. The inn later was renamed West Baden after the German city Wiesbaden.

Both sites underwent numerous physical and ownership changes over the years. Two moments stand out that made the region a nationally known destination. A 1901 fire destroyed West Baden, prompting owner Lee Sinclair to commit to building a grander facility that would be not only fireproof but also an engineering marvel. After several architects turned him down, he found one who agreed to build an octahedron-shaped building with an unsupported dome. When the hotel opened in 1902, journalists hailed it as the Eighth Wonder of the World.

In 1905 politician and hotelier Thomas Taggart launched a huge expansion of French Lick Springs, including a golf course and convention hall that served as unofficial Democratic Party headquarters. It is where Franklin D. Roosevelt came in 1931 wooing support for his 1932 presidential campaign.

The hotels enjoyed their heyday in the 1920s, when as many as fourteen trains a day dropped guests at the hotel door, and gambling and prostitution flourished—though not on hotel property itself. At one point fifteen illegal casinos operated in the valley.

The biggest business for Taggart was not gambling, but distribution of Pluto Water, sold over the counter at drugstores everywhere. By 1919 sales exceeded $1.2 million. (The water is no longer available because it contains lithium, classified as a controlled substance in 1971.)

The stock market crash brought hard times to the valley. French Lick managed to stay afloat thanks to an elite guest list that returned yearly; West Baden was acquired by the Jesuits in 1934 for use as a seminary and by Northwood Institute in 1966 as a hospitality arts college. In 1983 the building was vacated and soon started to collapse.

In the late 1990s, Indiana Landmarks spearheaded a $500 million restoration of both properties. In 2003 the Indiana legislature and Orange County voters approved a casino to be located between the two hotels to boost tourism. Today, the Cook Group owns both hotels and the casino, and the valley is enjoying a renaissance—this time with legal gambling.

Directions: From points north, take Indiana 37 south to Paoli, then take Indiana 56 west for about ten miles.

MORTON KEPT STATE IN LINCOLN'S CORNER DURING CIVIL WAR

Ask historians to name Indiana's greatest governor, and most will have the same answer: Oliver P. Morton.

He was the first governor born on Hoosier soil. He played a critical role during the Civil War backing the policies of President Abraham Lincoln and supplying troops for the Union army. He was driven more by principle than political considerations and because of that was not always popular.

"Morton was a polarizing figure who many people liked or disliked," said Ball State University history professor Ronald V. Morris, who owns and is restoring the home in Centerville where Morton lived and practiced law prior to becoming governor.

"He was a person dealing with issues in society that were very similar to issues we wrestle with today. I am not sure I would want him as a friend, but I certainly would not like him as an enemy," said Morris.

Indiana historian James H. Madison called Morton "the most powerful, important and controversial governor in Indiana's history."

Morton seemed destined for a life in politics. His full name was Oliver Hazard Perry Throck Morton, after Oliver Hazard Perry, a naval hero of the War of 1812 credited with the famous line, "We have met the enemy and they are ours."

Morton was born in 1823 in Salisbury on Indiana's eastern border. After the death of his mother in 1826, he went to live with his grandparents on a farm in Springfield, Ohio. He returned to Indiana at age fifteen, attended a city school in Centerville, and briefly clerked for a doctor. He enrolled at Ohio's Miami University, where he determined to become a lawyer.

Originally a Democrat, Morton joined the new Republican Party in 1856 because he felt more comfortable with its positions on slavery. He ran for governor that year and was defeated.

Opposite: The epitaph on Oliver Morton's gravestone reads, "He loved his country's good, with a respect more tender, more holy and profound, than his own life."

OLIVER PERRY MORTON

AUGUST 4, 1823,
NOVEMBER 1, 1877,

HE LOVED
HIS COUNTRY'S GOOD, WITH
A RESPECT MORE TENDER,
MORE HOLY AND PROFOUND,
THAN HIS OWN LIFE.

MORTON

In 1860 Morton was elected lieutenant governor on the Republican ticket with Henry S. Lane. When Governor Lane left after two days in office to serve as U.S. Senator, Morton was elevated to governor. Three months later, the Confederate attack on Fort Sumter launched the Civil War. Morton quickly proved to be one of President Lincoln's best recruiters, with Indiana supplying the second highest percentage of troops to the Union cause. Only New York had more.

In the midterm elections of 1862, Democrats took control of the Indiana General Assembly, in part due to Hoosier discomfort with the war's duration and distrust of Lincoln's abolitionist agenda. Democrats introduced a bill to reduce Morton's authority over the Indiana militia. In response, Republican lawmakers bolted to Madison to deny a quorum. With the legislature unable to pass a budget, Morton kept government operating by obtaining loans from friendly bankers.

Democrats called Morton a dictator, comparing him to the likes of Julius Caesar, Oliver Cromwell, and Charles I. Though certainly unconstitutional, Morton defended his actions as necessary in a state filled with Southern sympathizers—known as Copperheads—whom he considered traitors.

With the military campaign decidedly favoring the Union by the fall of 1864, Morton was reelected by a 20,000-vote margin. Soon after, Morton suffered a debilitating illness that caused partial paralysis from the hips down.

Despite his disability, Morton was chosen in 1867 to complete Lane's term as U.S. Senator and was reelected to the post in 1873. While on Senate business on the Pacific Coast in the summer of 1877, the paralysis spread to other parts of his body. He died on November 1, 1877, and was buried in Crown Hill Cemetery in Indianapolis.

Directions: Oliver P. Morton is buried in Lot 37, Section 9, of the Crown Hill Cemetery, 3400 Boulevard Place, Indianapolis.

HOOSIERS RESPONDED TO LINCOLN'S CALL

"Left camp at 9 o'clock. Rained all last night. Bad roads, slavish traveling today. Snowed all day, stalled several times. . . . Traveled 10 miles."

Private Albert S. Underwood of Parke County, Indiana, wrote those words on January 18, 1864, as he moved south toward Tennessee with the Ninth Battery, Indiana Light Artillery, during the final phase of the Civil War. There were no skirmishes that day. Nothing remarkable to note in his diary. Just walking in the snow to an uncertain destination.

Underwood was among 208,367 Indiana men who fought for the Union, and one of more than 25,000 who died in the cause. He was killed in early 1865 along with most of his unit when the boiler on the steamer *Eclipse* exploded on the Tennessee River in Kentucky.

His journal, available at the Indiana Historical Society William Henry Smith Memorial Library, is an intimate reminder of the toll the war took on ordinary Hoosiers. It is a leather-bound, three-inch by five-inch pocket diary with "1864" inscribed on the cover, its pages brittle and its handwriting barely legible in faded pencil.

Such diaries were common among Union soldiers, who wrote of weather, daily mileage, and food rations—almost anything but the politics that plunged the nation into Civil War on April 12, 1861, with the Confederate bombardment of Fort Sumter.

On April 15 President Abraham Lincoln called for 75,000 volunteers, hoping to end the South's rebellion in ninety days. In Indiana 22,000 men reported—three times the quota established by the U.S. War Department.

Historians attribute Indiana's high enlistments to patriotic instinct more than anything else. Hoosiers were not interested in the divisive issues of the day, according to Richard Nation and Stephen Towne in their book *Indiana's War*. The book noted, "When Hoosiers marched to war, most did not do so to end slavery. They marched to preserve the Union."

With Governor Oliver P. Morton at the helm, Indiana remained solidly pro-Union for the war's duration, and Indiana regiments played significant roles from Antietam to Vicksburg.

The Colonel Eli Lilly Civil War Museum depicts Indiana's role in the Civil War on the home front and on the battlefield.

Far from the main theater, Indiana itself was the site of occasional border raids from the Kentucky side of the Ohio River. On July 8, 1863, Confederate general John Hunt Morgan crossed the river at Brandenburg, Kentucky, and headed with 2,000 troops to the former Indiana capital at Corydon.

On July 9 a hastily gathered fighting force of 450 confronted Morgan's men outside Corydon but could not hold off the advancing cavalry. Union colonel Lewis Jordan, recognizing the odds, surrendered.

Morgan's men raided Salem, Dupont, Versailles, and other small towns before crossing into Ohio, where they were captured on July 26. Today, Hoosiers can follow their path by driving the 185-mile John Hunt Morgan Heritage Trail. The route runs through seven Indiana counties and is marked by directional signs and twenty-seven roadside point-of-interest displays.

Although the Battle of Gettysburg in July 1863 represented a turning point for the North, the war dragged on for almost two more years before the South surrendered. Recruiting became difficult, even in patriotic Indiana. About 18,000 Hoosiers went to war as a result of three separate drafts, a much lower percentage than the national norm.

The story of Indiana's critical war role is told at the Colonel Eli Lilly Civil War Museum in the Soldiers and Sailors Monument in Indianapolis. Exhibits illustrate the life of an ordinary soldier, from the mustering of troops to the soldier's return home.

Directions: The Colonel Eli Lilly Civil War Museum is located in the lower level of the Soldiers and Sailors Monument, 1 Monument Circle, Indianapolis.

INDIANA AFRICAN AMERICAN REGIMENT ENGAGED AT "CRATER"

Even before Indiana began recruiting them, African American Hoosiers volunteered to fight in the Civil War.

An 1862 act of Congress allowed President Abraham Lincoln "to employ as many persons of African descent as he may deem necessary and proper for the suppression of this rebellion." The Emancipation Proclamation of January 1, 1863, expressly allowed use of African Americans as combat soldiers.

Racial prejudices initially kept Indiana from enlisting blacks so the future soldiers went elsewhere. About 150 black Hoosiers signed up for the Massachusetts Fifty-fourth Infantry, memorialized in the Oscar-winning film *Glory*. Others crossed into Ohio, which assembled a regiment in the summer of 1863.

Late that same year, Indiana governor Oliver P. Morton realized the impact of out-of-state enrollments on Indiana's quota obligations. Morton authorized a black battalion and warned that "recruitment of colored troops in this state for companies or regiments organizing in other states is henceforth positively prohibited."

The Twenty-eighth Regiment, U.S. Colored Troops, organized at Indianapolis from December 24, 1863, through March 31, 1864. More than five hundred men trained at Camp Fremont near Fountain Square in Indianapolis on farmland loaned by abolitionist Calvin Fletcher.

Assigned to the Ninth Army Corps under Major General Ambrose Burnside, the regiment headed east—destined for intense action. The regiment first saw combat that June near White House, Virginia. Next, the Twenty-eighth accompanied General Philip Sheridan's cavalry through the Chickahominy swamps to Prince George Court-house and sustained "severe losses from frequent skirmishes with the enemy," as reported by Adjutant General W. H. H. Terrell.

In the summer and fall of 1864, the regiment took part in the siege of Petersburg, Virginia. Its most notorious assignment came on July 30 at the Battle of the Crater, where Union troops dug a tunnel under a Confederate fort. Soldiers carrying 8,000 pounds of gunpowder entered the tunnel in an ill-fated effort to blow up the Confederate defense. "Instead of victory there was disastrous defeat," according to *The Indiana Historian*. "When the mine explosion created the 'crater,' there was great disorder, and many Union soldiers were killed or wounded." Burnside was relieved of command for his role in the disaster.

The victims included eighty-eight members of the Twenty-eighth. "The colored troops went as far as they were ordered to go, and did just what they were told to do," observed the regiment's chaplain, Reverend Garland White, whose accounts of the war were published in a church newsletter.

Following that battle, Indiana raised four more companies to fill the regiment's depleted ranks. They joined the Twenty-fifth Corps, Army of the James, and were among the first to enter the fallen Confederate capital of Richmond, Virginia, in April 1865. The men's final duty was in Texas where, even after the surrender at Appomattox, Confederate units resisted Union victory

The Twenty-eighth mustered out of service on November 8, 1865, after proving its mettle and losing 212 men to battle or disease. The group was honored with a public ceremony in Indianapolis on January 8, 1866. The *Indianapolis Daily Journal* reported, "The occasion was a very pleasant one, and was a large nail in the great platform of equal justice."

Directions: This historic marker is located at the intersection of Virginia Avenue and McCarty Street south of downtown Indianapolis.

A block of restaurants and retail shops occupy the old Camp Fremont site where the Twenty-eighth Indiana organized and trained.

INDIANA STATE FAIR PROMOTED FARM INNOVATION

Not much has changed since the first Indiana State Fair in October 1852. Farmers showed off their finest specimens of cows, hogs, horses, and chickens. A Mechanics Hall displayed the newest reapers and plows. Corn growers competed for a silver cup for the heartiest ears. And right outside the main entrance, a vaudeville act performed three times a day under a big tent.

In 1851 the Indiana General Assembly established a State Board of Agriculture to encourage Indiana farming. The board promptly made a decision that has benefited Hoosiers ever since: An annual state fair would be held to demonstrate the latest farm equipment and to advance knowledge about soil, crops, and livestock.

The Indiana Farmer, a weekly newspaper, reported on the inaugural fair in its November 1, 1852, edition with a dispatch from L. Bellman: "Well reader, here we are at Indianapolis to witness one of the most interesting exhibitions ever made in the state. What a mass of people! And what a confusion of sound. The merry laugh is almost unheard in this neighing of horses, and braying of mules and Jacks, and lowing of cattle, and beating of sheep, and grunting of hogs."

From the get-go, the fair featured a lot more than farm animals. Although the term freak show is verboten today, it was a marketing ploy then. That very first fair advertised a "Giant" and "Giantess" and a two-headed calf.

From there, the fair expanded. In 1853 farmers exhibited squash as big as sheep, the largest weighing 185 pounds. In 1854 organizers threw a grand agricultural ball. In 1916 fairgoers rode a 2,000-foot high-speed roller coaster for the first time. In the 1920s the fair became the showplace for young Hoosiers enrolled in 4-H, an agricultural education program. Harness racing, the high school marching band, and "the world's largest boar" title were added along the way.

The fair's most momentous occasion ironically had nothing to do with agriculture but with a rock group that hailed from Liverpool, England. The Beatles performed two sold-out shows for 30,000 screaming fans on September 3, 1964, generating global headlines. Indianapolis was the band's tenth stop in a twenty-four-city tour, the only one at a state fair.

The historic horse barns near the Fairgrounds entrance were built during the New Deal by Works Progress Administration employees.

Indiana claims the sixth oldest fair in the country. The first was in New York in 1841, but credit for the idea goes back to a Massachusetts farmer named Elkanah Watson, who staged a "cattle show" in 1810 to demonstrate new breeds of livestock. The idea evolved into county agricultural societies with annual fairs, which grew into the state fairs we know today.

Until 1892 the Indiana State Fair rotated from city to city—places easily accessible by road, canal or rail. Some of the earliest took place in Lafayette, Madison, New Albany, Fort Wayne, and Terre Haute.

When it became clear that only Indianapolis could draw large enough crowds to be profitable, the capital city was chosen as permanent site and land acquired at Thirty-eighth Street and Fall Creek Parkway. In 1990 the Fairgrounds became a year-round event venue hosting conferences, concerts, and exhibitions. The duration of the fair has grown too, from five days in 1852 to seventeen days since 2009.

Directions: The Indiana State Fairgrounds is located at the corner of East Thirty-eighth Street and Fall Creek Parkway in Indianapolis.

PURDUE'S LAND-GRANT ORIGINS STILL APPARENT

Purdue University Boilermakers can thank the Morrill Land Grant Act for their highly regarded college diploma.

The law, signed by President Abraham Lincoln in 1862, gave federal land to states if they agreed to use the proceeds to start colleges of agriculture and mechanical arts for the children of the working class.

With the Morrill Act's passage, one historian noted, "higher education in the United States was no longer confined to its earlier classical, elitist beginnings." This was crucial for the nineteenth-century economy, which stood at a crossroads in the early days of the Civil War. North and South clashed on the battlefield and in their visions of the country's economic future : Would it be plantation based and built on the backs of slave labor or a diverse mix of farming and manufacturing based on the latest innovations in both?

In 1869 Indiana legislators selected Tippecanoe County for this new institution, thanks in part to a $150,000 startup gift from the school's namesake, John Purdue. Purdue was a Pennsylvania native who moved to the Lafayette area in the 1830s and made a fortune in dry goods, real estate, banking, and railroads.

The first classes were held in 1874 with six instructors and thirty-nine students. Over time extension offices were set up in all ninety-two counties, offering ordinary Hoosiers educational opportunities in agriculture, family life, and environmental sciences. Curricula expanded, too, encompassing aeronautics, veterinary science, and business and technology. Today Purdue enrolls close to 40,000 undergraduate and graduate students at its West Lafayette and regional campuses and employs more than 3,000 faculty members.

"John Purdue would be amazed by the size and scope of Purdue today, especially by its global reach," said Mitch Daniels, current Purdue president and former Indiana governor. "At the same time, he would recognize that the core mission remains the same: making education accessible and taking knowledge to the public as a way to better serve our state, nation and the lives of citizens."

University Hall was dedicated in 1877 and is the only building that survives from the original six-building Purdue campus. It houses the Department of History.

Purdue was one of forty-eight colleges created by the original Morrill act. A second act, passed in 1890, targeted Southern states whose economies had yet to recover from the Civil War. Thanks to both Morrill acts and subsequent legislation, 105 land-grant colleges operate today.

Even Purdue's mascot—the Boilermaker—can be tied to its land-grant roots. In the 1890s Purdue had just begun to field athletic teams that could compete against the dominant private colleges of the day, such as Wabash, Butler, and DePauw. In the 1891 football season opener, Purdue scored a 44–0 victory over Wabash, prompting the Crawfordsville newspaper to declare that the men of Wabash had been "snowed completely under by the burly boiler makers from Purdue."

The reference underscored the working-class origins of so many Purdue students, some of them whose parents made actual boilers, the source of steam that powered the new industrial economy.

It is an image still relevant today, Daniels observed: "We continue to believe it is our role to open the gates of higher education to all, not just to the privileged, and to concentrate on the skills and discoveries that build a great country and a great economy."

Directions: From I-65, go west toward Lafayette on South Street. Proceed for four miles and cross the Wabash River into West Lafayette. Visitor parking is at the Grant Street Parking Garage, 101 North Grant Street, West Lafayette.

ELI LILLY FOUNDED INDIANA'S BEST-KNOWN BUSINESS

From the time he was a youngster, Eli Lilly was fascinated by pharmaceuticals.

At age sixteen he served as an apprentice at the Good Samaritan Drugstore in Lafayette, Indiana. During the day he stocked shelves, washed bottles, and ran errands. At night he pored over the *United States Pharmacopoeia* to learn everything he could about mixing drugs.

By age twenty, Lilly had earned a certificate of proficiency in the field. Next he opened a drugstore on Greencastle's town square. It was the first of several career moves that prepared him to launch Eli Lilly and Company, today a multinational corporation with 39,000 employees and $20 billion in annual sales.

Lilly could not have foreseen the life-saving medicines his firm would pioneer for diabetes, cancer, cardiovascular disease, and depression. But he understood the recipe for success: develop products based on solid research, apply strict quality control to production, and limit distribution to doctors rather than door-to-door salesmen.

"He would be very pleased the company still bears his name and is still very viable," said company archivist Michael C. Jarrell. "I think he'd be proud of his legacy and the work we have done."

Born in Maryland in 1838, Lilly moved as an infant with his family to Kentucky, and as a teenager to Greencastle, where his father enrolled him in Indiana Asbury College, now DePauw University.

His career had barely begun when the Civil War erupted in 1861. Lilly served with distinction in the Union army. In 1862 he organized the Eighteenth Indiana artillery battery that played critical roles in the Chattanooga-Chickamauga campaign. As captain, Lilly received commendation for the capture of the Confederate depot at Tullahoma. His battery "expended 350 rounds, disabled at least two Confederate cannons and suffered no loss of men or guns," according to one account.

After a brief stint with the Ninth Indiana Cavalry that led to his detention as a prisoner of war, Lilly served out the war in the South. In June 1865 he was promoted to colonel, a title that became permanently attached to his surname.

ELI LILLY AND COMPANY ARCHIVES

After the war Lilly pursued entrepreneurial ventures with different partners and varying success. His personal life also had ups and downs. In 1866 his wife, Emily, died from a brain condition, leaving him the single father of a five-year-old boy, Josiah K. Lilly. The Colonel remarried in 1869 and the couple had a daughter, Eleanor. (She died of diphtheria at age thirteen.)

Encouragement from an Indianapolis businessman convinced Lilly to go into business for himself in 1876. At age thirty-eight, he opened a small manufacturing plant in downtown Indianapolis. The company outgrew the space and moved twice, settling in the southside industrial district where it remains today.

In its first year, Lilly offered a groundbreaking product: gelatin-coated pills. "This was a huge advancement considering that the standard forms of medication of the day were foul-smelling putrid liquids and bitter powders eaten off squares of paper," noted Robert L. Shook in the book *Miracle Medicines*.

Within five years sales exceeded $80,000. In 1881 the company incorporated and issued stock. In 1886 it hired a pharmaceutical chemist and a botanist to work on product quality.

Lilly died in 1898 at age sixty, but the company thrived under the leadership of his son and grandsons, Eli and Josiah K. Jr. Within twenty-five years of its namesake's death, Lilly began mass production of insulin to treat diabetes. This development more than any other made the company globally famous—a lifesaving endeavor the Colonel would have deemed the pinnacle of success.

Directions: The historic photo (above, left) shows Eli Lilly and Company's original brick building at 15 West Pearl Street, Indianapolis. Today a plaque (above, right) marks the spot where "Colonel Eli Lilly founded the Lilly Laboratories in 1876."

THE FAMOUS, INFAMOUS, AND HUMBLE LAID TO REST AT CROWN HILL

It is the nation's third largest cemetery and a "Who's Who" of Hoosier heroes. One president, three vice presidents, and eleven governors are buried there.

The grave of poet James Whitcomb Riley occupies the highest point—the crown hill—and is one of the most popular tourist sights in Indianapolis. So is the less grandiose burial place of bank robber John Dillinger, an Indianapolis native who became nationally known in the late 1920s as Public Enemy Number 1.

Crown Hill Cemetery, incorporated as a nonprofit institution in September 1863, reveals Indiana's history in a way few landmarks can rival. Federal judge and former congressman Albert S. White put it this way at the cemetery's dedication in 1864, "Let it be the glory of Crown Hill that the rich and poor, the proud and humble, alike may enter here." Some 400 people attended the dedication on June 1, 1864. A band played anthems, local preachers delivered prayers, and a poet read a few verses.

The first burial took place the next day. Lucy Ann Seaton was the young wife of an army captain who died from tuberculosis, the leading cause of death in the United States at that time. The prayer of her husband appears at the base of the stone, "Lucy, God grant I may meet you in heaven."

Another early burial was Josephine Jones, the fourteen-year-old daughter of an African American gravedigger. "From the beginning, Crown Hill was a place of racial and economic diversity," observed Douglas A. Wissing, coauthor of *Crown Hill: History, Spirit, Sanctuary*, published on the occasion of the cemetery's sesquicentennial.

The oldest remains are those of pioneers, most originally buried at City Cemetery (renamed Greenlawn and closed in 1890) and transferred to Crown Hill after city officials declared the first graveyard unsuitable for a growing population.

In 1866 approximately 700 Union soldiers who died in the Civil War and had been interred at Greenlawn were transferred to Crown Hill and reburied on land subsequently bought by the federal government for use as a national cemetery. In 1933 remains of 1,616

A wreath-laying ceremony is held every summer at the grave of President Benjamin Harrison to commemorate his August 20, 1833, birthday.

Indianapolis teenager Mitchell Amstutz poses next to the John Dillinger grave during a research trip to Crown Hill Cemetery.

Confederate soldiers who had been prisoners of war at Camp Morton in Indianapolis were moved to a Confederate Mound, also national cemetery property.

Landscape architect John Chislett of Pittsburgh designed Crown Hill, intentionally mixing elements of a nature park with burial plots to create a peaceful, inspiring setting.

More than 200,000 people have been buried or entombed in mausoleums at Crown Hill. Most prestigious is Benjamin Harrison, the twenty-third president of the United States, who is buried alongside First Lady Caroline Harrison in Section 15, Lot 37.

Adjacent to the Harrisons is author/playwright Booth Tarkington, winner of two Pulitzer Prizes. Business leaders include Lyman S. Ayres, who founded the L. S. Ayres Department Store in 1874; Eli Lilly, who launched the pharmaceutical company of the same name in 1876; and banker William H. English, who built the English Hotel and Theater. Sports figures range from Edward "Cannonball" Baker, who won the first race at the Indianapolis Motor Speedway and drove in the first Indy 500, to Robert Irsay, who brought the Baltimore Colts to Indianapolis in 1984.

Crown Hill Cemetery was added to the National Register of Historic Places in 1973. A list of notables buried on the grounds is available at: http://www.crownhillhf.org/docs/CrownHillNotables_lastname.pdf

Directions: The main entrance to Crown Hill Funeral Home and Cemetery is at 700 West Thirty-eighth Street, Indianapolis. Public tours start at the southern entrance at Thirty-fourth Street and Boulevard Place.

LEW WALLACE: HOOSIER RENAISSANCE MAN

Upon the death of Lew Wallace, the *New York Times* struggled to sum up, in a single headline, the seventy-seven-year-old Hoosier's accomplishments. The newspaper finally declared, "Won fame in many ways."

Wallace, his 1905 obituary noted, "achieved widespread distinction as a lawyer, legislator, soldier, author and diplomat" and was a man of "exceptionally refined manner, broad culture and imposing personal appearance."

It was quite a résumé for someone who at age six lost his mother to consumption, hated school, gave fits to teachers, and spent much of his life in small-town Crawfordsville, Indiana.

By the time of his death, Wallace was internationally known, an Indiana Renaissance man whose celebrity was comparable to General Dwight D. Eisenhower after World War II, evangelist Billy Graham in the 1960s and 1970s, and author J. K. Rowling after *Harry Potter and the Sorcerer's Stone* combined.

"I think his greatness lay in his ability to see the critical center of an issue, his personal integrity and willingness to address difficult issues, and his fearless curiosity," said Larry Paarlberg, director of the General Lew Wallace Study and Museum in Crawfordsville.

Born in Brookville in 1827, Wallace first came to the nation's attention during the Civil War, commanding troops in the Tennessee battles of Fort Donelson, Fort Henry, and Shiloh. In 1864 he was promoted to commander of the Eighth Army Corps and saved Washington, D.C., from a Confederate assault at the Battle of Monocacy.

Following the war, Wallace served as a judge at the trial of those who conspired to assassinate President Abraham Lincoln and presided over the trial of Henry Wirz, commander of the infamous Andersonville prison where thousands of Union soldiers died.

In 1878 President Rutherford Hayes appointed Wallace to be Governor of the New Mexico Territory. In 1881 Wallace became U.S. minister (what is known as ambassador today) to Turkey.

Although impressive, none of these distinctions brought him the

The bronze sculpture of Wallace on the museum grounds is a duplicate of the marble original by Andrew O'Connor displayed in the U.S. Capitol.

acclaim that came from *Ben-Hur*, his novel published in 1880 that told the story of Jesus Christ through the eyes of a Jewish noble condemned for a crime he did not commit.

Ben-Hur was the best-selling novel of the nineteenth century, translated into twenty languages, and still available today in a mass-market edition. It was made into a movie in 1925 and remade in 1959, starring Charlton Heston, a production that broke box-office records

Wallace's study, which he designed himself, is a blend of Romanesque, Byzantine, and Periclean Greek architecture.

and won eleven Academy Awards. A new version, with actors Jack Huston and Morgan Freeman, was scheduled for a 2016 release.

Wallace did most of his writing of *Ben-Hur* under a beech tree on the property of the Crawfordsville home he occupied from 1868 until his death. Although the house was sold outside the family and remodeled beyond recognition, much of the original Wallace property remains. The carriage house, Wallace's personal study, and a three-and-a-half acre arboretum have been preserved as a museum and natural space open to the public.

Wallace himself designed the study as a place to read, write, and entertain. Around the exterior, a limestone frieze features hand-carved faces from Wallace's books, including *Ben-Hur*'s Judah Ben-Hur and Tirzah.

Paarlberg labels the study "a nineteenth century man-cave" that brings Wallace's many passions to life. Wallace is one of two Hoosiers honored with a statue in the U.S. Capitol in Washington, D.C. (The other is Governor Oliver P. Morton.) A copy of the statue is on the museum grounds adjacent to the study.

Directions: The Lew Wallace Study and Museum is at 200 Wallace Avenue, Crawfordsville. For access to the main entrance and parking lot, follow the brick wall around the block to Elston Avenue.

RAILROADS TRANSFORMED INDIANA'S LANDSCAPE

Study a map from the late nineteenth century and it is easy to see how Indiana became known as the Crossroads of America. Like spokes on a bicycle wheel, railroad lines extended from Indianapolis in twelve directions. Tracks crossed the state from Lake Michigan to the Ohio River, Terre Haute to Richmond, and everywhere in between.

"By 1880, the steam railroad had triumphed over all other forms of transportation in Indiana," said historian Clifton J. Phillips in his book, *Indiana in Transition, 1880–1920*. The network of rail lines linked Indiana to major markets of the Midwest: Chicago, Cincinnati, Cleveland, Louisville, Pittsburgh, and Saint Louis.

The rise of the railroad is the story of Indiana's economic development. Trains carried passengers, of course, but more importantly they carried freight: corn, coal, tobacco, petroleum, and lumber, to name a few. And they did so more efficiently than boats or wagons.

Canals had proven financially impractical. In Indiana they were plagued by frequent flooding, freezing in winter, and costly maintenance of locks, gates, and bridges.

Roads were not much better. Imagine the challenge of transporting Indiana limestone, weighing 150 pounds per cubic foot, in a wagon on a macadam trail. Riding on flatcars, slabs could be hauled almost anywhere—and they were: to North Carolina for the Biltmore Estate, to New York for the Empire State Building, and to the nation's capital for the Washington National Cathedral.

By the time railroads came to Indiana, the technology was not new. Steam power developed in the eighteenth century in England, where the world's first public passenger steam train ran in 1825. In the United States, the Baltimore and Ohio Railroad was the first commercial passenger and freight service, chartered in 1827, and still operates today as CSX Corporation.

Indiana's first major steam railroad, completed in 1847, was an engineering marvel. The Madison and Indianapolis line, eighty-six miles long, climbed a steep hill just north of Madison on its way to Indianapolis. European visitors and Hoosiers alike were impressed by the ease with which a train of cars, pulled by a British engine, made the ascent.

Railroad enthusiasts can see a full-size replica of a train depot at the Monon Connection Museum, as well as G-scale model train running on 1,200 feet of stainless-steel track.

With that success, rail construction exploded. In 1850 Indiana had 200 miles of completed track. By 1880 that number had grown to 4,000 miles of track traversing eighty-six of the state's ninety-two counties.

Railroads transformed villages into thriving towns and cities almost overnight. North Judson in Starke County is one example. At one point, 125 trains a day passed through the community on four different rail lines including the Chesapeake and Ohio, Erie, New York Central, and Pennsylvania. Today, Hoosiers can relive the experience by riding a vintage caboose at the Hoosier Valley Railroad Museum in North Judson.

Perhaps Indiana's most famous railroad was the Chicago, Indianapolis and Louisville, a combination of several early lines running north to south through Indianapolis and nicknamed the Monon from a Potawatomi Indian word meaning "swift running." The Monon transported Union troops, ammunition, food, and medicine during the Civil War. In April 1865 a Monon engine pulled President Abraham Lincoln's funeral train at five miles per hour from Lafayette to Michigan City.

During the heyday of railroads, about 1,500 depots dotted the Indiana landscape. Today, fewer than 250 are still standing, including this one in Clinton, Indiana, in Vermillion County.

The Monon Connection Museum houses a large private collection of railroad memorabilia, including dining car china, lanterns, and brass steam-locomotive bells and whistles.

Although the interstate highway supplanted railroads in the twentieth century, Indiana's economy still relies on 3,884 miles of active track. Indiana ranks in the top ten states for employment, wages, and freight tonnage related to railroads.

Directions: The Monon Connection Museum is one and a half miles north of Monon, Indiana, on US 421.

GENE STRATTON-PORTER: AUTHOR AND NATURALIST

Henry David Thoreau, John Muir, and John Burroughs. To this list of famous American naturalists, add the name Gene Stratton-Porter of Indiana.

Decades before the modern environmental movement began, Stratton-Porter warned against human activities that could lead to climate change. A best-selling fiction author, too, Stratton-Porter brought the beauty of the earth to the masses through her nature books, photographs, essays, and poems.

Barbara Olenyik Morrow, in her biography *Nature's Storyteller,* observed that Stratton-Porter took readers "to a place where many had never been or where they wanted to return—to flowering meadows and clean-smelling woods and marshes alive with birdsong."

Stratton-Porter was a native Hoosier, born in 1863 and raised in Wabash County by parents who loved the outdoors and all of God's creatures.

As a child, Geneva Grace Stratton spent hours bird watching on the 240-acre family farm called Hopewell. As an adult, she intensely studied birds, moths, and flowers, photographing and drawing them, writing about them, and working for their preservation.

She was supported in her pursuits by her husband, whom she wed in 1886 and who called her Gene. Charles D. Porter was an Adams County businessman thirteen years her senior. At first the couple lived in his hometown of Decatur, but the neighborhood did not suit Gene.

After the birth of their daughter, Jeannette, the family moved to Geneva, where Stratton-Porter worked with architects to design a grand two-story "cabin" with Wisconsin cedar exterior and a colonnaded porch. The home was dubbed Limberlost after the nearby Limberlost Swamp blanketed with wildflowers and swarming with wildlife. It was an ideal laboratory for her nature studies, and it was from here that Stratton-Porter launched her writing career at age thirty-six.

Her first published piece in 1900 was an article in *Recreation* magazine lamenting a fashion trend of the day: women's hats trimmed with bird feathers. Her first novel, *A Song of the Cardinal,* was the story of a lovesick bird that found his mate.

This view of the Cabin at Wildflower Woods is from the rear of the property, where a thirty-five-bed, one-acre garden is tended to attract birds and butterflies. The front looks out on the waters of Sylvan Lake.

It was her fourth novel, published in 1909, that brought Stratton-Porter international fame. *A Girl of the Limberlost* tells the story of a poor but determined girl who sold moths and caterpillars to pay for her schooling. When the story opens, the girl is at cross-purposes with her widowed mother; by book's end, the relationship is restored and the girl has found romance and happiness.

Although some critics panned Stratton-Porter's works as saccharin, readers loved them. From 1910 to 1921, five of her novels made the top ten bestseller list for fiction. The author was so wealthy that, when she decided to change scenery again in 1914, she bought land in her own name and paid for the construction of a house herself.

The draining of the Limberlost Swamp for commercial purposes had destroyed much of the habitat she used as inspiration. Her new home, the Cabin at Wildflower Woods on Sylvan Lake, offered 120 acres of fields, woods, and gardens for an outdoor workshop. Today, both Limberlost and Wildflower Woods are operated by the Indiana Department of Natural Resources as historic sites open to the public.

In 1919 Stratton-Porter went to California to pursue movie production opportunities and never returned full time to her husband or Indiana. She died in a car accident in 1924. Some years after her death, her descendants arranged to have her body moved back to be buried amidst the flora and fauna of Wildflower Woods.

Directions to Limberlost: The Limberlost State Historic Site connects with US 27 in east-central Indiana. The address is 200 East Sixth Street, Geneva.

Directions to Wildflower Woods: The Gene Stratton-Porter State Historic Site is at 1205 Pleasant Point, Rome City, on the southwest side of Sylvan Lake.

A BETTER PLOW, THANKS TO SOUTH BEND'S JAMES OLIVER

Though his name is not nearly as familiar as John Deere's, James Oliver of South Bend, Indiana, revolutionized agriculture with his invention of a new type of plow.

An 1878 advertisement for the Oliver Chilled Plow boasted: "Buy no other. Will last for years, and no blacksmith's bill to pay. It is the only guaranteed chilled plow made."

That was not hyperbole. At its height, Oliver's company produced three hundred plows a day, exporting them to such faraway places as Japan, Germany, and Mexico.

The story began in Scotland, where James was born in 1823, one of nine children raised by George and Elizabeth Oliver. "An older brother and sister had immigrated to America, and they sent letter after letter home begging the rest of the Oliver family to come," said Travis Childs, director of education at The History Museum in South Bend. They did come, when James was twelve.

Reports of cheap land and jobs lured some of the Oliver family to Saint Joseph County, where James demonstrated an intense work ethic. He cut and sold wood, did menial chores, and worked as a farm hand. He cast molds at a foundry. He packed flour into wooden barrels at a gristmill. He mastered carpentry skills in a cooper's shop.

In 1847 Oliver went to work for the Saint Joseph Iron Company, which made plows and castings. All of these experiences prepared him to become South Bend's leading industrialist. In 1855 he invested in a foundry that made cast-iron plows, and began looking for a way to make a better one.

Plows, of course, are as old as agriculture itself, necessary to turn and break up soil to make it arable. The standard plow consists of two main parts: a moldboard, the curved piece that lifts up and turns over the sod, and the blade that does the cutting, known as the plowshare.

OPPOSITE: The restored boiler house and smokestack from the old Oliver Chilled Plow Works add historic ambience to the new Oliver Industrial Park on Chapin Street.

An outdoor exhibit tells the story of James Oliver and his chilled plow.

In Oliver's day, both cast iron and steel were used, but steel was scarce and expensive and cast iron was soft. That caused dirt to stick to the moldboard, forcing farmers to stop every few minutes to clean it.

In 1857 Oliver received his first patent for "An Improvement in Chilling Plowshares." A chill is a mold that cools liquefied metal rapidly, making the metal harder on the surface. Over the course of several decades, Oliver obtained forty-five patents aimed at producing sharper and firmer cutting edges while maintaining flexible, more break-resistant turning pieces.

In 1871 the *South Bend Register* observed, "If he keeps on improving his plow it will soon have no rivals in the country." To keep up with demand, the Olivers opened a new factory complex in 1876 with five buildings, 400 employees, and a 600-horsepower Harris Steam Engine to power the machinery.

After Oliver died in 1908, his son, J. D., took over the company and directed two more decades of innovation. J. D. and his family lived in close proximity to the factory in a thirty-eight-room mansion called Copshaholm. Today the house is open to the public as part of the South Bend museum complex that includes the Studebaker National Museum and The History Museum.

One indication of the chilled plow's success, James Oliver's son, J. D., built this lavish mansion for his family in 1896. It was designed by New York architect Charles Alonzo Rich.

Changing economics forced the Olivers to take the company public in the late 1920s. Stockholders approved a mega merger that kept the Oliver name alive in tractor and tool production for some time; it was subsumed in a series of consolidations and plant closings in the 1970s. The South Bend factory closed in 1985; its smokestack and boiler house still stand in a new industrial park named after the man who changed the face of plowing.

Directions to Oliver Mansion: Tours of the Oliver Mansion begin at The History Museum, 897 Thomas Street, South Bend.

Directions to Oliver Industrial Park: The Oliver Plow Industrial Park is on Chapin Street between Western Avenue and Sample Street in South Bend.

COVERED BRIDGES RARE SIGHT ON INDIANA LANDSCAPE

Like an heirloom jewel passed down through generations, covered bridges are Indiana's most threatened inheritance.

From 1835 through the 1920s, more than six hundred covered bridges were built in the state. "Only 89 are still standing today," according to the Indiana Covered Bridge Society, which works to preserve and restore them. Of those still standing, some carry traffic, others have been bypassed or relocated, and five are on private property.

Indiana lost most of its covered bridges before communities realized they were worth saving. They were blown down, burned down, torn down, or replaced by newer structures made with steel and concrete.

Starting in the 1970s preservationists worked to get surviving bridges on the National Register of Historic Places, giving them a degree of protection from intentional demolition. Like anything fragile, they are still vulnerable—to fire, floods, vandalism, and bad driving.

The first covered bridge in the United States was built over the Schuylkill River at Philadelphia by the famed New England bridge builder Timothy Palmer. It was dubbed the Schuylkill Permanent Bridge because, up to that time, folks wanting to cross the river had to take a ferry or use a floating pontoon bridge. Its completion in 1805 ignited a covered bridge building craze. "Immediately wooden bridges all over America added coverings, and new bridges planned were thenceforth designed as covered bridges," said historian Eric Sloane in the American Geographical Society's July 1959 journal.

The building of the National Road through the middle of Indiana launched the state's covered-bridge era, with the first one erected in Henry County in 1835, according to the Indiana Historical Bureau.

Two of the top builders were J. J. Daniels and Joseph A. Britton, who lived near Rockville, explaining the concentration of covered bridges in Parke County, which calls itself the Covered Bridge Capital of the World. Starting the second Friday in October, Parke County hosts an annual ten-day festival with special tours of its thirty-one bridges—the most of any Indiana county.

Visitors to Turkey Run State Park can walk across—or float under—the two-lane Narrows Covered Bridge, built by J. A. Britton in 1882.

Why were bridges covered? "To keep them dry," explained Karin Woodson, curator at the Parke County Historical Society Museum. Wood rots rapidly when exposed to rain and snow. Covering bridges kept moisture out of the joints, prevented sagging boards, and protected the floors from becoming slippery.

A friendly competition between Indiana's Medora Covered Bridge and the Cornish Windsor Covered Bridge in New England has yet to determine which is the nation's longest. Medora, which crosses White River's east fork in Jackson County, claims to be longer with a clear span of 430.4 feet. That is the length of the bridge between abutments. The bridge was built in 1875 and closed to vehicles in 1972.

The Cornish Windsor, which crosses the Connecticut River between New Hampshire and Vermont, claims to be longer at 449.5 feet based on the length of its lattice truss, which extends past the abutments. It is two lanes and still open to car traffic.

Bridgeton in Parke County claims to have the state's "most famous covered bridge" because it crosses a waterfall. The 267-foot bridge, once the most photographed bridge in the state, was destroyed by arson in 2005. Citizens came together and built a replica the following year that is almost identical to the original built in 1868 by Daniels.

Directions: The Narrows Covered Bridge is accessible from Turkey Run State Park in Marshall, Indiana, located southwest of Crawfordsville.

KING COAL FUELS INDIANA

Coal is to Indiana what oil is to Texas. Since the mid-1800s, it has been the fuel that powers the Hoosier economy.

"We get 85 percent of our energy from coal," said Bruce Stevens, Indiana Coal Council president. "That's huge because Indiana is the number one manufacturing state in the nation."

A fossil fuel millions of years in the making, coal is essentially combustible rock formed by dead plant material. Some is near the surface and easily obtained through strip mining. The rest is deep beneath the earth and must be mined underground. Southwest Indiana has plenty of both.

Although coal was discovered in the 1700s along the banks of the Wabash River, there was no organized effort to mine it until 1825 in Warrick County, according to *Indiana in the Civil War Era* by Emma Lou Thornbrough.

In the 1830s Perry County had the first of many "company towns" whose existence depended on coal. Miners employed by the American Cannel Coal Company, along with their families, lived in cabins owned by American Cannel and did all their shopping at a company-owned store.

An early study identified eighteen counties in Indiana with sizable coal reserves, extending south from Vermillion County to the Ohio River and stretching from Posey County to Perry County along the state border. In 1873 Governor Oliver P. Morton proclaimed that the vast mineral wealth in these counties was "more valuable than the gold and silver mines of California, Colorado or Nevada."

He was right. By 1900 coal was the country's fuel of choice, used to power steamships and railroad engines, to generate electricity, and as an essential ingredient for making iron and steel (Indiana coal is not suitable for metallurgy so the Northwest Indiana steel industry had to buy its coal elsewhere). In 1950 the U.S. Geological Survey reported that the value of coal production in Indiana exceeded $100 million, more than that of all other natural-resource industries combined.

Aja Mason, a retired coal worker, is curator at the Museum of the Coal Industry, which occupies the site of a former coal mine in Lynnville.

A display of protective helmets worn by miners through the years.

In the second half of the twentieth century, demand for coal nationally began to fall as trains switched from coal power to diesel fuel and homes converted to oil or gas furnaces. Starting in the 1970s, the federal government set rules on air quality that required coal-fired plants to install cleaning equipment to reduce pollutants released into the atmosphere. This especially affected Indiana coal, which has high sulfur content and is dirtier than the coal found in western states.

Today natural gas is displacing coal as an energy source in much of the country, but not Indiana, which is the nation's second largest consumer of coal behind Texas. In 2014 fifteen companies operated underground and strip mines in ten counties employing 2,370 Hoosier miners and producing 39 million tons. As for the future of the industry, Stevens said it depends on environmental rules imposed by the government and technological innovations.

The Museum of the Coal Industry in Lynnville in Warrick County maintains an extensive collection of mining equipment, safety helmets, union memorabilia, and other items documenting the history of coal in Indiana. Visitors can climb aboard a switcher locomotive that picked up coal cars at the Peabody Lynnville Mine, sit at the control panel of a 3270 dragline built for AMAX Coal, or walk through a replica company store. The museum maintains a memorial wall remembering those who have died while on the job, a recognition that coal mining—despite modern safety enhancements—remains as one of the most dangerous occupations in the country.

Directions: The Museum of the Coal Industry is located on Indiana 68, one mile west of Lynnville in Warrick County.

JAMES HINTON: INDIANA'S FIRST AFRICAN AMERICAN LAWMAKER

James Sidney Hinton, a Union army veteran and Republican Party orator, was a nineteenth-century torchbearer for civil rights who became the first African American elected to the Indiana General Assembly.

Hinton achieved these accomplishments during an era of fundamental social and political change, and at a time when blacks in the Hoosier State faced much of the same racial prejudice as those living in the South.

Indiana's 1816 Constitution prohibited slavery and indentured servitude, making it a free state, yet few white Hoosiers were willing to accept racial equality. The revised state constitution of 1851 prohibited black migration into Indiana; other laws kept blacks from voting, sending their children to public schools, or testifying in a trial involving white citizens.

"Indiana was often described as being one of the more Southern of the Northern states because of its laws that openly oppressed and discriminated against African Americans," said historian Wilma Moore. "James Hinton plays an important and significant role in Indiana political history."

Hinton was born on Christmas Day in 1834 to free black parents in Raleigh, North Carolina. His father, John Cook Hinton, was a successful businessman. His mother, Hannah (Mitchell) Hinton, was a piano teacher and active with the Methodist Episcopal Church. The family moved to Terre Haute around 1848 when James was still a teen. He attended schools organized and taught by African Americans.

Hinton worked as a teacher and a barber, then moved to Indianapolis around 1860 and opened a "real estate and intelligence office," according to historical records.

Because blacks were prohibited from joining the military in Indiana, Hinton volunteered for military service in Massachusetts after the Civil War erupted. He served as a recruiter for the Massachusetts Fifty-fourth and Fifty-fifth U.S. Colored Regiments and returned to Indiana in 1863 to assist with the organization of the Twenty-eighth U.S. Colored Troops, according to Moore.

Following the war, Hinton, a staunch Republican, stumped on behalf of the "party of Lincoln" to black voters in Alabama, Georgia, Indiana, Mississippi, and Tennessee. It was during these travels that Hinton advocated for educational opportunities for black children, and for public funds to be allocated for schools and teachers.

He served as a presidential elector-at-large and was one of two black delegates to the Republican National Convention in 1872. In 1874 he became the first African American to hold statewide office when he was appointed trustee of the Wabash and Erie Canal.

His greatest political achievement was his election to the Indiana General Assembly in 1880, just ten years after ratification of the Fifteenth Amendment giving black men the right to vote. "Thirty years ago, the Indiana Legislature was engaged in concocting brutal laws to prevent the entrance of colored people into this state," proclaimed the *Indianapolis Leader*, a black newspaper, after Hinton's election. "Now a member of the race then proscribed is a member of the Legislature. Time sets all things right."

Hinton served one term. He was the first of four blacks to serve in the legislature in nineteenth-century Indiana. The others were James M. Townsend of Richmond, elected in 1884; Richard Bassett of Howard County, elected in 1892; and Gabriel Jones of Indianapolis, elected in 1896.

Directions: The Hinton memorial is on the second floor of the Indiana Statehouse, 200 West Washington Street, Indianapolis.

OPPOSITE: A bronze bust of James Hinton was dedicated on January 16, 2014, during a ceremony at the Indiana Statehouse.

"LET US BE CONSISTENT IN ALL OF
OUR ACTIONS, ASKING NOTHING FOR
OURSELVES WHICH WE ARE NOT
WILLING TO YIELD TO OTHERS."

QUOTED FROM "SPEECH DELIVERED BY J. S. HINTON"
AT WOOD'S HILL, VIGO COUNTY, INDIANA, JULY 4, 1876.

JAMES SIDNEY HINTON
1834-1892

Throughout his life, James Sidney Hinton dedicated himself to achieving equal rights for African Americans. Hinton was born in North Carolina; his family moved to Terre Haute, Indiana during the 1850s. Hinton settled in Indianapolis and during the Civil War recruited black men to serve in the United States Colored Troops.

In 1880, Marion County voters elected Republican James Hinton to Indiana's House of Representatives. He was the first African American to serve in the State House. After his term in the legislature, Hinton traveled throughout the state and from Missouri to Washington, D.C. as he campaigned for civil rights. James Hinton died on November 6, 1892.

INDIANA CAPITOL A GATHERING PLACE FOR HOOSIERS

The most poignant moments in Indiana history have taken place under its dome and on its front steps. Suffragettes lobbied for the right to vote. Mourners filed past the casket of President Benjamin Harrison to pay their last respects. Actress Carole Lombard raised the American flag and sold war bonds the day before her untimely death in a plane crash. Union members jammed the halls to protest repeal of a prevailing wage law.

From its official opening in 1888 to the Indiana bicentennial in 2016, the Statehouse has been a gathering place for Hoosiers of all political stripes.

The three branches of government have offices there: executive, legislative, and judicial. So does the news media. In a way, so does the public.

During the legislative session, citizens observe action from the balconies or hallways. Groups schedule Statehouse space for meetings, award ceremonies, receptions, rallies, and displays. Tours set off from the information desk near the rotunda from 9:00 a.m. to 3:00 p.m. daily.

"The Statehouse belongs to everyone, and as long as the metal detector allows you in, you have the right to absorb as much of its majesty as you can take," said Greencastle High School English teacher Donovan Wheeler, who takes his seniors on a field trip to the capitol every year.

The first thing visitors are reminded is that Indianapolis was not the original state capital. Corydon claimed that distinction until 1825, when the legislature moved the seat of government to Indianapolis in order to be closer to the population center, which had gravitated north in the years following statehood.

The Indiana General Assembly at first met at the Marion County Courthouse while other state offices operated out of houses and storefronts.

The legislature approved construction of a capitol in 1832 to be built on the south end of the present site, facing Washington Street. Completed in 1835 for $60,000, this Statehouse was made of brick,

Monroe, Lawrence, and Owen Counties provided the limestone used in building the capitol.

wood, and stucco in Greek Revival style with porticos on both ends modeled after the Parthenon.

In 1867 the ceiling of the House chamber collapsed. Although it was repaired, lawmakers worried about the building's long-term safety. In 1877 the legislature passed a law authorizing construction of a new capitol with the process to be overseen by a Board of Statehouse Commissioners at a cost not to exceed $2 million.

The board held a contest to select the architect and chose Edwin May from Indianapolis out of more than twenty submissions. May's design drew heavily on the national capitol—a classical Renaissance Revival style with a central, domed rotunda and the House and Senate chambers on opposite sides.

May died in 1880. His draftsman, Adolph Scherrer, succeeded him as supervising architect. Legal and contractual disputes and limestone delivery problems delayed the project from time to time; nonetheless it was finished in 1888 slightly under budget to the delight of legislators.

Although construction was still under way, the general assembly convened there on January 6, 1887, and discovered "a monumental, stately and fireproof edifice," with Corinthian columns and grand

Artificial lights placed behind the rotunda dome's stained glass ensure the colors are visible even on cloudy days.

courts with skylights and abundant natural light, wrote James A. Glass in *The Encyclopedia of Indianapolis.*

During the twentieth century, the Statehouse was repeatedly remodeled to accommodate an increase in government employees in a way that detracted from the building's interior aesthetics. In 1988, for its centennial, the Statehouse underwent an $11 million renovation aimed at restoring much of the building's original historic atmosphere.

Directions: The Indiana Statehouse is located at the corner of Capitol Avenue and Washington Street in downtown Indianapolis.

NATURAL GAS DISCOVERY PROVED FLASH IN THE PAN

It was Indiana's version of the Gold Rush. In the 1880s, the discovery of a massive natural gas field in east-central Indiana launched a gas boom of historic proportion. The news spread fast—as it did with California gold—and folks poured into Indiana in search of fortune.

"There was so much gas here people thought it would last forever," said Jerry Long, president of the Gas City Historical Society, which operates a museum dedicated to the town's colorful past.

That misguided belief led to wasteful practices. Residents burned "flambeau" lights twenty-four hours a day, seven days a week on city streets and set wells afire just to see how high the flames would go.

By 1910, however, the boom was over, and places such as Gas City would never be the same.

The story of Gas City is typical of the communities that found themselves located in what was believed to be the largest natural gas field in the world. Before the boom, "our town was a little hamlet of three hundred people called Harrisburg," Long noted.

In 1892, in an effort to capitalize upon its newfound resource, the city changed its name to Gas City and began an all-out marketing blitz to attract industry.

The Gas City Land Company, incorporated that same year, acquired land around the original town plat of Harrisburg and subdivided it in order to sell plots to homeowners and businesses. At their most ambitious, town fathers forecast a population of 25,000.

The company offered economic-development incentives that make today's tax abatement packages look like chump change. Manufacturers that committed to Gas City qualified for free land, free water from the Mississinewa River, and free natural gas for fuel and lighting "in unrestricted, unlimited and inexhaustible quantities," as stated in advertising circulars.

Glass companies were especially eager recipients because of the vast amounts of natural gas required to fire their furnaces. Within two years, Gas City was home to five glass plants, including a green-glass bottling business, a tin-plate factory, an iron and steel works, and a strawboard manufacturing plant.

Jerry Long, president of the Gas City Historical Society, shows off colored-glass dinnerware manufactured at the end of the nineteenth century by the U.S. Glass Factory in Gas City.

A building boom accompanied the industrial activity. Construction workers put up a bank, hotel, and opera house. Newcomers lived in tents and shanties while awaiting housing.

In 1900 Gas City reported a population of 3,622—twenty-five times larger than in 1890. And then, all of a sudden, the gas was gone. By 1902 low pressure affected most of the wellheads. By 1913 Indiana was importing natural gas from West Virginia to meet demand.

In Gas City, only two factories survived the loss of the wells: Thompson Bottle Works and United States Glass, both which closed during the industrial decline of the 1980s.

In contrast to the Gold Rush, most Hoosier boomtowns did not become ghost towns. Gas City, Marion, Portland, Kokomo, and others persevered and "used the industrial foundation bestowed by natural gas to lure additional factories and commerce," James A. Glass noted in an article in the *Indiana Magazine of History*.

A visitor to Gas City cannot help but notice tokens of the town's glory days. Street signs in the shape of gas derricks line Main Street. The grandest homes date to the days when business owners got rich quick off liquid gold.

The only gas derricks left in Gas City are the decorative street signs that line Main Street.

Gas City's population holds steady at 6,000—twice what it was during the gas boom—and its proximity to Interstate 69 makes it an attractive site for the logistics sector. In 2007 retail giant Wal-Mart opened a distribution center on the east side of town big enough to house sixteen football fields.

Directions: The Gas City Museum is open on weekends at the corner of Grant and West North A Street in Gas City.

AMISH THRIVING IN NORTHERN INDIANA

In an era of declining church membership for most Christian denominations, one group of believers is experiencing healthy, unprecedented growth.

In 2014 the estimated Amish population in Indiana exceeded 50,000, according to the Young Center for Anabaptist and Pietist Studies at Elizabethtown College. That number is larger than the cities of Columbus, Jeffersonville, or Kokomo, and more than double the Amish population of fifteen years ago.

"They are growing. It would be fair to describe them as thriving," said Jerry Beasley, executive director of Menno-Hof, an interpretive center in Shipshewana that tells the story of the Anabaptist religion. That includes both the Amish and Mennonite denominations, which emerged from the same Reformation-era movement in Europe and ascribe to adult baptism and strict separation from the affairs of state.

The trends defy what is happening in the general population, which is less likely to connect with formal religion than in generations past. A 2015 Pew Research Center survey found that 28 percent of first-year college students reported no religious affiliation at all, up 12 percentage points since the question was first asked in 1971.

Beasley says it is a matter of mathematics: "The Amish continue to have large families, and they have been fairly effective in retaining the children in the church."

Although Indiana Amish are spread throughout the state, the largest concentration is in Elkhart and Lagrange Counties, where the population has grown from 5,000 in 1964 to close to 23,000 today. It is the third largest settlement in the United States after Lancaster, Pennsylvania, and Holmes County, Ohio. It is also the state's oldest Amish community, dating to the 1840s when families in pursuit of more farmland moved west from Pennsylvania and Ohio.

For most Hoosiers, a horse and buggy driving alongside cars on rural highways is the most familiar symbol of Amish life, a reflection of the religion's desire to live simply without influence of modern possessions that would create inequality among members. For the same reasons, the Amish generally forbid higher education, dress in plain clothes, and avoid using telephones or the Internet.

Menno-Hof is a nonprofit visitor center with information about the faith and life of Amish and Mennonites.

Far from being reclusive, however, Indiana's Amish are significant contributors to the economies where they reside and to a thriving tourist business around Shipshewana in Lagrange County and Nappanee in Elkhart County.

"Farmland is very difficult to get and hard to find," Beasley observed. "The Amish have diversified their activity for earning a living." Many own businesses, work in retail shops, or are employed in factories, in particular Elkhart's recreational vehicle industry, which provides one of every four jobs in the region.

Increasing contact with the outside world might appear a threat to Amish life, but a 1992 research project found the opposite was true. As explained by sociologist Thomas J. Meyers, "If they all had to farm with horses, there would be far fewer Amish men today. . . . There simply is not enough land for all young people to begin married life on farms."

In 1988, in an effort to tell their story to the general public, members of the Amish and Mennonite churches opened Menno-Hof in Shipshewana, a museum-like center with interactive exhibits that tell the story of their faith.

Tourists wanting to immerse themselves in the culture can visit Amish Acres in Nappanee, which preserves the Stahly-Nissley-Kuhns farmstead settled by German immigrants circa 1840. The site features the Round Barn Theatre, which perennially presents the show *Plain and Fancy*, a musical comedy about the customs, morals, and unique attire of the Amish.

Directions: The Menno-Hof center is at 510 South Van Buren Street in Shipshewana.

Horse-drawn buggies are a familiar sight in Elkhart and Lagrange Counties, where they travel on the shoulder alongside automobiles.

BENJAMIN HARRISON: AN ACTIVIST PRESIDENT

Although his name does not show up on lists of greatest presidents, Benjamin Harrison did more during his one term in office than some better-known presidents accomplished in two. Consider the following:

He expanded the U.S. Navy to both coasts and strengthened its fleet, which had no working battleships when he took office.

Fulfilling a campaign pledge, he signed into law the Sherman Antitrust Act, landmark legislation that outlawed monopolistic business practices.

He was a conservationist before environmental protection was popular. He lobbied for and signed the 1891 Forest Reserve Act and used it seventeen times to set aside 13 million acres in the western United States for national forests.

He opened Ellis Island, advocated for African American voting rights, commissioned the Pledge of Allegiance, and convened the first modern Pan-American Conference.

The only president elected from Indiana, Harrison was a man of action who believed in energetic and transparent government.

"He wasn't a Hoosier by birth, but by choice," noted Charles A. Hyde, president of the Benjamin Harrison Presidential Site. "And Indiana could not have had any president more closely aligned with its altruistic values. In typical Hoosier fashion he diligently went about his work, quietly doing what was right for the right reasons and never seeking undue recognition."

From a young age, Harrison seemed destined for a life in politics. His great-grandfather, Benjamin Harrison V, signed the Declaration of Independence; his grandfather, William Henry Harrison, was the first governor of the Indiana Territory and ninth president of the United States; and his father, John Scott Harrison, the only American to be both child and parent of a president, represented Ohio in Congress.

Harrison was born and educated in Ohio; he moved to Indiana with his wife, Caroline, in 1854 to start a legal career. While building his business, he held a variety of court positions and in 1860 was elected Indiana Supreme Court Reporter.

Visitors mingle outside the Italianate red-brick home that Benjamin and Caroline Harrison built in 1875 and from which he conducted a front-porch campaign for president in 1888.

When the Civil War broke out, Governor Oliver P. Morton personally called Harrison into service. Immediately commissioned a lieutenant, Harrison raised a regiment of one thousand volunteers and rose to rank of brigadier general by war's end. As in other aspects of his life, Harrison led by example. Harrison the officer would fix coffee in the middle of the night and take it to enlisted men shivering on the picket line.

After the war, Harrison resumed his law practice, built a three-story, sixteen-room home on the north side of Indianapolis, and became deeply involved in Republican Party politics. From 1881 to 1887, he served as a U.S. senator. In 1888 he secured the GOP nomination for president, emerging as a consensus candidate at the national convention because he was most delegates' second choice in a field of seven.

Four times in U.S. history a candidate won the election but lost the popular vote. It happened in 1888. Although the incumbent Democratic President Grover Cleveland received 90,000 more votes, Harrison carried the Electoral College 233 to 168 and was inaugurated on March 4, 1889.

Four years later, Cleveland got his revenge. Historians say a combination of circumstances cost Harrison re-election. He had refused to curry favor with party bosses, so they were a bit lukewarm about his second candidacy. His wife was fatally ill during the campaign. Harrison suspended his efforts, and she died two weeks before the election.

His personal loss weighed heavily upon him, but not the electoral defeat. He said laying down the burdens of the presidency was like being released from prison. Harrison returned to his home in Indianapolis, resumed his law practice, and married again. Visitors to the Benjamin Harrison Presidential Site can see much of the home's original furniture and artwork, including the rosewood and satinwood bed in which Harrison died in 1901 at the age of sixty-seven.

Directions: The Benjamin Harrison Presidential Site is at 1230 North Delaware Street, Indianapolis.

INDIANA MIAMI DENIED FEDERAL RECOGNITION

In 1897 an assistant attorney general made a legal error that cost the Miami Nation of Indiana its federal recognition as a tribe. The Miami have been fighting ever since to win it back.

"Our people are as upset now as they were one hundred years ago," declared Chief Brian Buchanan. "We are not giving up."

It is a story that began not long after Indiana achieved statehood, when settlers came flooding into the state with their eyes on land already occupied by Potawatomi, Delaware, Miami, and other Indian nations. The government's formal policy was removal. Under the Indian Removal Act of 1830 and a succession of treaties, Indiana's Native Americans were pushed west to present-day Kansas and Oklahoma.

The Miami fought to stay in Indiana during the nineteenth century and were split in two when the U.S. government forcibly removed about half of them in 1846. Under an 1840 treaty, the Miami ceded virtually all of its commonly held land in exchange for $550,000 in annuity payments.

Through this treaty and earlier ones, several individual Miami were awarded land, and they and their families were exempted from removal, forming the nucleus of the Miami Nation of Indiana. Those sent to Kansas eventually relocated to Oklahoma and today are called the Miami Tribe of Oklahoma, one of 566 federally recognized tribes.

For decades the Miami of Indiana were treated by the government like their western Miami counterparts, exempt from federal taxes, free to hunt and fish without a license, and eligible to attend federal Indian schools.

Immediately following removal, Miami lands in Indiana were illegally taxed. Hoping to recover past payments, the Miami appealed to the Department of the Interior, which oversees tribal matters through its Bureau of Indian Affairs. The case was referred to Assistant Attorney General Willis Van Devanter, a Hoosier who would go on to become a Supreme Court justice.

As part of his decision on the tax case, Van Devanter concluded that the Indiana Miami were "no longer a tribe" under a law called the Dawes Act and were U.S. citizens, thus ineligible for tribal recognition—a decision the government later admitted was based on a flawed

Elders of the Miami Nation of Indiana kick off the 2015 June Powwow with the Grand Entry ceremony.

application of the law.

Within four decades of his decision, the remaining Miami lands in Indiana virtually disappeared. Indiana Miami could no longer attend federal Indian schools, exercise their treaty rights, or continue many important cultural practices, including speaking their language.

In 1978 the Department of the Interior set up a new process for acknowledging Indian tribes. The Indiana Miami applied for recognition but were denied on grounds they could not prove continuous existence of a tribal community with a functioning political system. They challenged the ruling in court without success. They have also asked Congress for legislation restoring their tribal rights but failed to muster enough support.

The Indiana Miami today operate on a barebones budget, sustained largely by private donations and bingo nights held at the Tribal Complex in the old Peru High School building.

Though its relationship to the federal government is fractured, the tribe's identity as a sovereign nation is intact. Tribal council meets monthly and holds a general meeting open to the public twice a year. An annual powwow is held every June at the Miami Living Village in Parke County, which features native drumming, singing, dancing, and storytelling.

Doctor Scott M. Shoemaker, director of the tribe's cultural and historic preservation office, said teaching the once dormant "Myaamia" language at summer camp and other venues has been a recent focus since it is through transmission of language that culture is passed on to newer generations.

Buchanan says members will continue to do what they can through the political system to win back their tribal recognition. He invites fellow Hoosiers to join them in the struggle by contacting their congressional representatives and by attending or financially supporting the many events sponsored by the Miami each year.

Directions: The Powwow takes place at Miami Living Village three miles east of Raccoon Lake State Recreation Area, 11515 East US 36, Rockville.

ELWOOD HAYNES: AUTOMOBILE PIONEER

The date was July 4, 1894. The location was the Pumpkinvine Pike, located three miles east of Kokomo, Indiana. Elwood Haynes had hauled his newfangled carriage—a horseless one, no less—to the edge of the city for a test drive. He unhitched the horses that towed it there, mounted the driver's seat, and with a push start drove into the future.

"The little buggy ran eastward, carrying three passengers about one and one half miles," Haynes later recounted. "It was then stopped and turned about when it ran all the way into Kokomo without making a single stop. Its speed was about seven miles per hour."

As a result of that day's accomplishments, Haynes claimed to have invented the first American automobile, dubbed the Pioneer. One or two others beat him to it, according to the Smithsonian Institution, but this much is certain: Haynes was one of the first U.S. inventors to build and sell gas-powered cars to the public.

The story is recounted at Kokomo's Elwood Haynes Museum on South Webster Street, which occupies the colonial-style home Haynes shared with his wife, Bertha, until his death.

There's much more to his story than cars, noted museum docent Pete Kelley: "His work in metallurgy changed the industrial world." Among his many discoveries, Haynes patented an alloy called stellite, a hard metal still used today in machine tools, medical equipment, cans, and cutlery.

Although Haynes is Kokomo's most famous celebrity, he is not a native son. Born in Portland, Indiana, in 1857, Haynes attended public school in Jay County before enrolling at Worcester Polytechnic in Massachusetts, a place that nurtured his scientific interests, and later at Johns Hopkins University in Baltimore.

Armed with curiosity and new understanding of chemistry, Haynes returned to Portland, where he worked in education and the booming natural gas industry and started thinking about ways to use gas to power a horseless carriage.

He moved to Kokomo in 1892 to manage a gas plant and pursued his idea for a buggy. His first step was to purchase a one-horsepower Sintz gasoline engine he eyed at the Chicago World's Fair. His second was to draw up a blueprint. His third was to persuade two brothers,

The Haynes-Apperson Company priced this 1905 Model L at $1,350 and marketed it as "a car that is always reliable." The car is displayed on the first floor of the Elwood Haynes Museum.

Elmer and Edgar Apperson, to take his idea and build him a car in their machine shop at forty cents an hour.

Following the successful test drive of the Pioneer on Pumpkinvine Pike, Haynes and the Appersons formed the Haynes-Apperson Automobile Company, which sold nearly a dozen cars its first year. In 1902 the partnership dissolved, with each continuing to make vehicles.

At its height in 1923, the Haynes Automobile Company produced forty cars a day, according to museum documents. Haynes died in 1925. With the economy facing an uncertain future, his wife dissolved the business soon after.

Haynes donated the Pioneer to the Smithsonian in Washington, D.C., in 1910, still believing that his car was the first. Smithsonian curators state in their exhibit documents that "there were other, earlier automobiles—including the Duryea which is in the museum's collection," a reference to an 1893 car built by Charles and Frank Duryea of Springfield, Massachusetts.

Haynes's significance in automobile history is undisputed. In July 2015 he was inducted into the Automotive Hall of Fame in Detroit, cited for his successful test drive of the Pioneer "two years before Henry Ford's Quadricycle and less than a year after Charles Duryea's Motorized Wagon."

Directions: The Elwood Haynes Museum is at 1915 South Webster Street in Kokomo, Indiana.

SOCIAL GOSPEL PASTORS BATTLED URBAN PROBLEMS

From his pulpit at Plymouth Congregational Church in Indianapolis, Reverend Oscar C. McCulloch missed no opportunity to push his congregation out of the pews and into the world.

"Here lies our work," he exhorted one Sunday, unveiling a vision of a church that educated, entertained, and provided role models to the "wretched" poor of the city.

"I want to teach the poor that their best friend is the Christ, and that all good is in His name," said McCulloch.

McCulloch, who served his congregation from 1877 to 1891, was one of the earliest and most influential proponents of a Protestant religious movement called the Social Gospel. A response to the negative effects of the Industrial Revolution, its purpose was threefold: to meet immediate needs of the suffering, to bring them to Jesus Christ, and to make government aware of its obligation to use policy to improve the lives of the less fortunate.

In Indiana's biggest cities, churches established rescue missions and hospitals. They opened settlement houses where immigrants could find temporary lodging and learn English. They supported workers' strikes and urged passage of temperance laws.

McCulloch used Sunday mornings to speak to the powerful about their obligation to humanity. His sermons focused on the relation of capital to labor, the exploitation of child and female workers, and unethical business practices. Outside church walls, he advocated better coordination of the charitable sector and served as president of the Indianapolis Benevolent Society and the Charity Organization Society.

Churches could do only so much to address social ills, McCulloch believed; he constantly lobbied the Indiana General Assembly for funding and regulatory action. In a sermon titled, "Some Things I Want the Legislature to Attend To," he urged free kindergarten, vocational education, and separating young offenders from hardened criminals.

Similar themes sounded from the sanctuary of Central Avenue Methodist Church in downtown Indianapolis. As early as 1877, Reverend Reuben Andrus urged his congregants to seek "cessation of wars, diminution of poverty, better clothing, better shelter, better food for the people, enlarged securities for health."

The former Central Avenue Methodist Church was the mega-church of the Social Gospel era, packing more than 1,300 congregants into the pews on Sunday.

In 1893 the women of Central Avenue created an outreach center for homeless girls and unwed mothers—a first-of-its-kind facility in the city. Called Door of Hope, the endeavor expanded to meet the needs of transient men and was renamed Wheeler Rescue Mission. In 1899 Reverend Charles Lasby pushed for funding of a Methodist hospital. Between World War I and the Great Depression, Reverend Orien Fifer preached about labor relations, child labor, and the evils of divorce—many of the same issues that consumed McCulloch.

Though McCulloch's Plymouth church was torn down in 1901, the congregation survived as First Congregational Church of Christ. It relocated to the city's north side and continues to be known as one of the city's most progressive congregations.

The preservation group Indiana Landmarks took over the vacant Central Avenue Methodist Church in 2011 and operates it today as its state headquarters. Tours are available most Saturdays in the summer.

The building's highlight is its dome-ceilinged Grand Hall, the former sanctuary, where as many as 1,300 parishioners packed the pews in the early 1900s, making it the largest Methodist church in Indiana.

"The center continues in many ways the traditions of the Social Gospel movement through its community outreach and by providing a multifunctional space which serves the whole person through music, art, community forums, lectures and celebrations," said Indiana Landmarks President Marsh Davis.

Directions: The Indiana Landmarks Center is at 1201 North Central Avenue in Indianapolis.

MAJOR TAYLOR WAS FASTEST BICYCLE RIDER IN WORLD

Dubbed the "colored cyclone" by newspaper reporters of the early 1900s, Hoosier Marshall W. "Major" Taylor was a champion cyclist whose speed was surpassed only by railway locomotives. Despite achieving international fame—and defying bigotry and Jim Crow segregationist practices—Taylor died penniless and alone at age fifty-three, a forgotten sports hero.

"Major Taylor's name should be like Jackie Robinson's. Sure Robinson broke down barriers in major league baseball, but Taylor, he broke down barriers in sports half a century earlier," said Lynne Tolman, president of the Major Taylor Association, Inc., a nonprofit group in Worcester, Massachusetts, a city Taylor adopted as his home.

"He was largely forgotten for much of the twentieth century," Tolman said. "We're working on turning that around."

Born in Indianapolis in 1878 to Saphronia and Gilbert Taylor, young Marshall was raised and educated for several years by a wealthy white family who employed his father as a coachman. The family gave him a bicycle.

When he was just thirteen, Taylor was hired to perform cycling stunts outside a bicycle shop. He likely earned the nickname "Major" because of the soldier's uniform he wore when he performed. Around the same time he won his first amateur race on a ten-mile road course.

While white promoters let Taylor compete in trick bicycle competitions, he was kept out of local riding clubs due to his race, "and many white cyclists were less than welcoming to the black phenom," according to Gilbert King in the September 2012 issue of *Smithsonian Magazine.*

In 1895 Taylor moved to Worcester with his employer and racing manager Louis "Birdie" Munger, who planned to build a bike factory there. He found people in the East more tolerant. "I was in Worcester only a very short time before I realized there was no such race prejudice existing among the bicycle riders there as I had experienced in Indianapolis," Taylor wrote in his 1929 autobiography, *The Fastest Bicycle Rider in the World.*

Major Taylor was known for his aerodynamic bicycle posture with his back flat and his eyes downward.

By 1898 Taylor held multiple world records. In 1899 he won the world one-mile professional cycling championship. He won U.S. circuit championships in 1899 and 1900.

From 1901 to 1904 he raced all over Europe, Australia, New Zealand, and the United States. He retired in 1910 at thirty-two. Along the way, "he encountered closed doors and open hostilities and faced it all with dignity. He'd go on the racing circuit, couldn't get a hotel room, a meal," Tolman said.

Although he made a great sum as a racer, Taylor had little success as a businessman. Debts and health issues tapped his savings in the 1920s. With a failed marriage, he moved to Chicago in 1930 and lived at the Young Men's Christian Association. His health deteriorated, and he died in 1932 in the charity ward at Cook County Hospital and was buried in a pauper's grave. Sixteen years later, a group of biking enthusiasts had his remains moved to a more honorable site at Mount Glenwood Cemetery in Glenwood, Illinois.

Taylor's Indianapolis hometown gave him belated recognition for his achievement, naming in his honor the Major Taylor Velodrome, a world-class bicycle racing track built in 1982. The track is home to the Marian University cycling team and hosts competitions, clinics, and open-ride sessions. It has the distinction of being the first building paid partly by taxpayers in Indianapolis to be named for an African American.

Directions: The Major Taylor Velodrome is located at 3649 Cold Spring Road down the road from Marian University in Indianapolis.

OPPOSITE: Cyclists take practice laps at the Major Taylor Velodrome in Indianapolis.

SPORTS HERO DAN PATCH NEVER LOST A RACE

He was the A. J. Foyt of harness racing. During a ten-year career, Dan Patch broke records and raked in prizes. His appearance at events drew fans by the thousands. Through it all, he never lost a race.

Sports writer Charles Leerhsen called Dan Patch "the most celebrated American sports figure in the first decade of the 20th century, as popular in his day as any athlete who has ever lived."

Leerhsen is the author of *Crazy Good: The True Story of Dan Patch, the Most Famous Horse in America.* Published in 2008, the book is testament to Dan Patch's reputation. Though few sports fans today recognize the Dan Patch name, his legend lives on in books, a movie, and in the town of Oxford, Indiana, where the mahogany-colored pacer was born in 1896.

Visit Oxford on a Saturday morning and you will find old-timers gathered for coffee at the Dan Patch Café. The water tower proclaims, "Home of Dan Patch." On the first weekend following Labor Day, the Lions Club sponsors Dan Patch Days, a festival featuring basketball and euchre tournaments, a car show, and a baby contest.

Visitors to Oxford, Indiana, cannot miss the farm where Dan Patch was raised and whose barn still proclaims his unofficial record in the mile.

The breaded tenderloin is a favorite on the menu of the Dan Patch Café in Oxford.

Raised by Daniel Messner Jr., Dan Patch began life as a knobby-kneed colt that could hardly stand to nurse. With perseverance, Messner raised him to be a pacer and entered him in his first harness race in Boswell, Indiana, where he won the mile in just two minutes and sixteen seconds.

Mention horse racing, and most Americans think of thorough-breds and the Kentucky Derby. Dan Patch was a standardbred, and his jockey rode behind him in a two-wheeled cart called a sulky.

After experiencing success in Indiana, Messner contacted a New York horse trainer to prepare Dan Patch for the 1901 Grand Circuit, harness racing's top events nationwide. He raced in Detroit, Cleveland, Columbus, and Buffalo, among other cities. His twelve-straight wins that year netted Messner $13,800 in prize money.

In 1902 Messner sold Dan Patch to M. E. Sturgis of New York City for $20,000, an unheard-of sum at the time. Sturgis turned around and sold the horse for $60,000 to Marion W. Savage, owner of the International Stock Food Company of Minneapolis.

By this point, other stables refused to race Dan Patch because of certain defeat, but he continued to build his legend by endorsing commercial products and by racing against the clock.

In Lexington, Kentucky, in 1905, he ran the mile in a record one minute, 55.25 seconds. The following year he clocked one minute and fifty-five seconds during an exhibition at the Minnesota State Fair. The new record did not become official because the sulky used a dirt shield, which was not allowed, but Savage took full advantage of the moment. He renamed his farm the International 1:55 Stock Food Farm.

Dan Patch retired to be a stud in 1909. Horse and owner died in 1916, but they were not forgotten.

The U.S. Harness Writers Association still gives out the Dan Patch Awards. The Hoosier Park Racing and Casino in Anderson is located on Dan Patch Circle, and the park's feature race for pacers is the Dan Patch Invitational.

It is unknown where Dan Patch was buried. Horse fans often stop to pay respects at a headstone and historical marker on the east edge of Oxford, where the farm where he was raised still proclaims his unofficial record on the side of the barn.

Directions: The Dan Patch historical marker is at 203 South Michigan Road near the intersection of Indiana 352 and Indiana 55 in Oxford, Indiana.

DRAINING OF KANKAKEE BASIN DESTROYED HABITAT

Long before scientists understood the benefits of wetlands, Hoosiers drained a wildlife Garden of Eden that stretched from western Saint Joseph County to the Illinois state line.

The Grand Kankakee Marsh was "one of the great freshwater wetland ecosystems of the world," according to the U.S. Fish and Wildlife Service. Nicknamed the Everglades of the North, it was a habitat for bass and walleye, passenger pigeons, woodpeckers, minks, and muskrats, to name just a few.

"It was a paradise," said Randy Ray, executive director of The History Museum in South Bend. "It was over 500,000 acres of marsh and flowing water; it was home to an unbelievable variety of plants and animals."

The sluggish Kankakee River created the marsh much like a leak in a wall dampens a basement carpet—gradually. The river followed 250 miles of bends and oxbows covering a point-to-point distance of about ninety miles. With a downhill slope of five inches per mile, water constantly seeped into adjacent soil, producing a giant, sponge-like prairie.

Before white men arrived, Native Americans used the marsh for fishing and hunting. In the 1830s the federal government acquired the land from the Potawatomi through treaties that pushed the Indians west. In 1850 Congress passed the Swamp Land Act giving the marsh to the state of Indiana so it could be made into arable land.

For several decades the marsh provided commercial and recreational fishing and hunting opportunities; it was a sportsman's paradise, attracting presidents, industrialists, and even European nobility who had heard stories of waterfowl so numerous they blackened the sky.

But farmers coveted the soil, which was a black, sandy loam, three to six feet deep, and ideal for crops if only the water could be removed. In 1882 the state's chief engineer recommended draining the entire wetland.

Dredge boats got to work, straightening more than 2,000 bends in the river and digging lateral ditches to carry runoff. By 1917 the entire

With abundant cattails and lily pads, the wetlands in the Jasper-Pulaski Fish and Wildlife Area resemble the Florida Everglades, much like the Grand Kankakee Marsh would have looked.

river had been reduced to a series of straight dredged ditches extending eighty-two miles from South Bend to the Indiana-Illinois state line.

The new farmland was among the most productive in the world, but the impact on wildlife was immediate. As one example, biologists estimated that the draining of the Kankakee River eliminated one fifth of the migratory bird population in the United States.

In the years since, the conservation movement has proven the critical role wetlands play in filtering and removing pollutants from water, reducing erosion of stream banks, and providing habitat for species that have become endangered. An award-winning public television documentary, *Everglades of the North—The Story of the Grand Kankakee Marsh,* has helped educate the public about the issue.

Efforts are ongoing to bring back some of the wetlands. In 1979 Lake County dedicated the Grand Kankakee Marsh County Park, restoring 920 acres of marshland.

The Indiana Department of Natural Resources operates several fish and wildlife properties entirely or partly within the Kankakee River basin with wetlands set aside for protection.

The Jasper-Pulaski Fish and Wildlife Area in Medaryville, Indiana, looks much like the Grand Kankakee Marsh would have appeared prior to drainage. Its shallow marshes provide an ideal stopover for migratory birds. Each fall thousands of sandhill cranes visit the region on their route south and can be seen right before sunset from a viewing platform at Goose Pasture.

Directions: The Jasper-Pulaski Fish and Wildlife Area is at 5822 North Fish and Wildlife Lane, Medaryville.

INDIANA IS NATION'S ROUND-BARN CAPITAL

Fulton County historian Shirley Willard calls round barns the "cathedrals" of the countryside. They are symbols of a bygone time in Indiana agriculture when farmers combined form, function, and aesthetics.

Their heyday was 1890 to 1915. Agricultural experts of the day advocated round barns as efficient and economical. Architect Benton Steele of Pendleton, Indiana, advertised them as "the cheapest and best from every standpoint" with their "ordinary joist frame construction, assisted by the new bending system."

Indiana has long claimed the title round-barn capital of the nation, with more round barns than any other state. From 1985 to 1988, the Indiana Round Barn Survey identified 226 structures in Indiana. Since then, tornados, fire, and aging have claimed more than half. As of 2015 approximately one hundred were still standing, Willard said.

The largest grouping is in Fulton, Marshall, Miami, and Kosciusko Counties. John T. Hanou, author of *A Round Indiana,* attributes the cluster to the experience and reputation of a single builder, C. V. Kindig and Sons, who put up almost all of the houses, barns, sheds, and corn cribs in three of those four counties.

In Marshall County, the Leland family built three almost identical barns with twelve sides and central silos. Farmer John Leland could do so himself because his brother was a carpenter.

George Washington is believed to have built the first round barn in the United States in 1792, actually a sixteen-sided barn used as a treading mill to thresh grain.

The Shakers were known for circular barns starting in the 1820s, the designs serving as a metaphor for life in the community. The top level served as a gathering place and hay room. On the main floor, livestock were kept in stanchions radiating out from a central grain bin, and hay could be dropped from the level above.

Today, both polygonal and circular barns are considered round barns but they are not the same. The perfect circle developed later as the result of balloon framing, an engineering advance that allowed for self-supporting roofs.

This round barn was built in 1924 and used to house farm animals. After a tornado took the roof off in 1989, its owner, Larry Paxton, donated it to the Fulton County Historical Society for use as a museum.

For several decades, Fulton County preservationists have been at the forefront of a movement to save round barns from extinction.

In 1989 Larry Paxton donated his round barn, damaged by a tornado, to the Fulton County Historical Society, which moved and restored it at its current location along US 31 four miles north of Rochester. In its second life as a museum, the barn displayed farm vehicles and implements from the early twentieth century. (In August 2015 straight-line winds during a thunderstorm tore off the barn's roof and damaged much of its contents—another harsh reminder of the vulnerability of these hallowed structures.)

In 1990 the society founded the National Round Barn Center of Information to keep track of the round barns in the United States and look for potential investors of those in danger.

As one example, the owner of a deteriorating round barn in Plymouth brought photos of it to the Fulton County Museum and offered to give it free to anyone who would save it. Willard contacted

The wooden joists of the barn's dome radiate in a kaleidoscope pattern from the cupola.

Nappanee's Amish Acres, whose owner not only restored the barn but converted it into a vibrant cultural center, the Round Barn Theater.

"While many round barns have been lost, several new ones have been built, including a horse training barn near Lafayette," Willard noted with pride.

For her and so many others in north central Indiana, saving round barns is a labor of love. "They're so beautiful," she said. "When you see one, you just say, 'Oh my goodness.'"

Directions: The Fulton County Historical Society and Museum is on US 31 four miles north of Rochester, Indiana.

INDIANA OPENED FIRST MENTAL HOSPITAL IN 1848

In 1848 the Indiana Hospital for the Insane opened on the west side of Indianapolis, launching a new era in health care that would witness the most progressive innovations and the most heinous abuses.

Historians credit the great social reformer Dorothea Dix with persuading Hoosier lawmakers to fund a mental hospital in order to provide more humane treatment to its most vulnerable citizens.

When Dix began her campaign in the early 1840s, society's understanding of mental illness was crude, if not primitive. Idiots and the insane, as they were called at the time, were often housed in county poor asylums or sent to live in foster homes funded, albeit inadequately, by the government. They were chained in closets or dungeon-like cellars with no sunlight and almost no human interaction.

In 1845 lawmakers authorized building a hospital, and the state purchased for that purpose a 160-acre farm two miles from downtown Indianapolis on the National Road.

The Indiana Hospital for the Insane opened on November 21, 1848, with eight patients. "This achievement marked the beginning of state responsibility which made possible medical care for the insane," wrote Evelyn C. Adams in the *Indiana Magazine of History*.

The site made medical history many times during its existence, noted historian Elizabeth Nelson, director of public programs at the Indiana Medical History Museum, located in the hospital's old pathology building. "There were certainly dark periods in the hospital's history," Nelson observed. "There were also very important innovations by progressive people in charge of the hospital."

Three innovators stand out:

William B. Fletcher, superintendent from 1883 to 1887, reduced the medicinal use of alcohol, halted secret burials of patients who died in state care, and abolished the use of physical restraints.

George F. Edenharter, superintendent from 1893 to 1923, recognized the value of research in understanding causes and treatments of mental illness and in 1895 opened one of the nation's first pathology departments, which engaged in groundbreaking research and medical instruction.

The Indiana Medical History Museum is the oldest surviving pathology facility in the nation and is on the National Register of Historic Places.

Max A. Bahr, superintendent from 1923 to 1952, sought to remove the stigma from the mentally ill. He prohibited lobotomies and instituted an occupational and recreational therapy program that engaged patients in rug weaving, sewing, basket making, checkers, pool, croquet, and tennis.

When the legislature authorized three more regional psychiatric institutions in 1889, the Indianapolis hospital changed its name to Central State. It remained the largest with an average population of 1,800 at its height in the early twentieth century.

During an active period of building expansion at the turn of the century, the hospital became much like a college campus, adopting Doctor Thomas Kirkbride's "linear plan," which featured a large central main building with flanking pavilions and patient rooms with windows looking out on aesthetically pleasing landscapes. Kirkbride was a leading national authority on mental illness who insisted that physical surroundings should be part of any treatment plan.

As with many state-funded services, mental health suffered from repeated cycles of public attention followed by woefully inadequate spending over the years, as well as chronic allegations of physical abuse, overcrowding, and improper treatment.

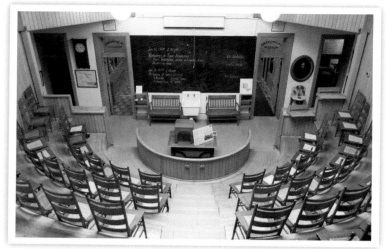

This teaching amphitheater used by the Indiana University School of Medicine is the centerpiece of the Indiana Medical History Museum.

The development of more effective drugs for treating mental illness led to the deinstitutionalization movement of the 1960s, and Central State discharged many of its long-term patients and became involved in community-based mental health. In the 1990s complaints of abuse and unnecessary deaths led to the closing of the facility by Governor Evan Bayh.

Although much of the original campus has been torn down, the pathology building was saved and became a museum in 1969. Appearing much as it did in 1895, the museum preserves patient autopsy records, tissue slides, and pathological specimens, including an impressive display of brains. Its focal point is the wood-paneled lecture hall illuminated by skylights used by the Indiana University School of Medicine until 1956.

Directions: The Indiana Medical History Museum is at 3045 W. Vermont Street in Indianapolis.

CARNEGIE LIBRARIES DISTINGUISH INDIANA LANDSCAPE

They are the libraries that Andrew built. In the early twentieth century, industrialist Andrew Carnegie funded the establishment of public libraries across the United States in an effort to bring the joy of reading and learning—free of charge—to the masses.

To Hoosiers' great benefit, Indiana received more Carnegie grants than any other state, $2.6 million in all, enough to build 164 libraries in 155 cities and towns from 1901 to 1922.

Drive through just about any community, and you will be able to see one. Although there is uniformity in their footprint, there is variety, too—in architectural style, building material, and personality. For example:

- The Wabash Carnegie Public Library was designed by Fort Wayne architect J. F. Wing and dedicated in 1903. It was constructed of Bedford limestone in neoclassical revival style with a stained-glass dome.
- The Whiting Public Library, opened in 1906, was designed by Bloomington, Illinois, architect Paul O. Moratz in an eclectic Romanesque Revival style.
- The Brownsburg library, made of brick in the Craftsman-Prairie style popularized by Frank Lloyd Wright, was designed by Indianapolis architect Norman H. Hill and dedicated in 1918.

Carnegie himself never explained why Indiana received so much of his largesse. David Kaser, distinguished professor emeritus, Indiana University School of Library and Information Science, suspects it was a matter of timing and greatest good.

By the time Carnegie launched his program, the eastern states were well stocked with libraries and had less need. The South and West were not organized enough to take full advantage of Carnegie's generosity. Indiana, Kaser noted, had financial need and was receptive to the benefits with its "bookish culture, widespread literacy . . . and sufficient experience with rental and social libraries to assure the extensive future use of free public libraries when they should become available."

In *Temples of Knowledge—Andrew Carnegie's Gift to Indiana*, author Alan McPherson said that Hoosiers were voracious readers in the early twentieth century, yet "Indiana's publicly funded township and county

The Carmel Carnegie Library houses Woodys Library Restaurant with upstairs dining, a downstairs neighborhood pub, and outdoor patio seating.

libraries were rather limited in literary selection, poorly housed and often meagerly staffed." Some were "subscription libraries," which meant patrons had to pay a monthly or annual fee to borrow books.

Carnegie, a self-made steel tycoon, wanted libraries that were free to all. To obtain funding from him, communities had to agree to provide a building site and levy enough taxes to maintain the building and its collection into the future. To take full advantage of Carnegie's generosity, the Indiana General Assembly in 1901 passed the Mummert Library Law, which allowed local units of government to do just that.

At the outset, communities could design the libraries as they pleased; after 1908 the Carnegie Corporation issued guidelines that standardized their cost and appearance. Steps typically led to the front door, a symbolic representation of Carnegie's philosophy that patrons should step up intellectually to get the most from the library experience.

Today, 106 of the 164 libraries Carnegie funded are still functioning libraries, many of them remodeled or expanded to accommodate customer demand and new technology. That fact would surely delight Carnegie, who called the taste for reading "one of the most precious possessions of life."

Thomas Jefferson's ten-foot bronze likeness greets visitors to Warder Park, the site of a Carnegie library built in 1905 in Beaux-arts classical style. Community leaders in Jeffersonville are contemplating a new use for the building, currently unoccupied.

Eighteen were demolished by human hands or natural disaster. The others have been adapted to new uses, including as museums, town halls, private homes, galleries, and even restaurants.

Directions: The Jeffersonville Carnegie Library building is in Warder Park at 109 East Court Avenue, Jeffersonville.

Directions: The Carmel Carnegie Library building is at 40 East Main Street, Carmel.

GARY: THE CITY THAT U.S. STEEL BUILT

In 1904 the directors of the U.S. Steel Corporation made a monumental decision for the future of northwest Indiana.

After considering locations in Illinois and Pennsylvania, they voted to build a steel plant on the southern shore of Lake Michigan. Easy access to water and rail and proximity to Chicago made it the obvious choice for what was to be the world's largest steel mill.

Before property owners in the area knew of the plan and could boost asking prices, the company purchased 9,664 acres of mostly swamplands and dunes. Almost overnight, construction workers transformed the landscape. They filled swamps, rerouted a river, dug a harbor, built a plant, and plotted a city with 4,000 residential and commercial lots.

Incorporated in 1906, this new city was named Gary—after Elbert H. Gary, U.S. Steel's board chairman.

The company's vision was to create a model of industrial efficiency, and the city's founding fathers reveled in the early nicknames conferred upon their creation: Magic City, Industrial Utopia, and City of the Century.

And for a while it was.

The lure of good jobs drew immigrants and African Americans by the thousands, ensuring that Gary would have a diverse population from the outset. By 1920 more than fifty nationalities were represented there.

Gary's public schools received national recognition for rigor and innovation. Educator William A. Wirt moved to Gary from Bluffton, Indiana, in 1907 to implement on a large scale his innovative "work-study-play" system with an eight-hour day and enriched course of study that exposed students to laboratory science, orchestra, swimming, and vocational training.

The restored Recreation Pavilion in Gary's Marquette Park is a tourist site today and symbolic reminder of the steel city's early-twentieth-century affluence.

INDIANA LANDMARKS

Parks and other cultural amenities figured prominently in the community's design. In order to ensure residents access to beaches, the city annexed lakefront to the east and created the 241-acre Marquette Park with views of both water and sand dunes.

Gary's population peaked in 1960 at 178,000, making it Indiana's second largest city after Indianapolis. That would soon change as a result of foreign competition in the steel industry, high labor costs, and the failure of the industry to modernize.

By the time Richard G. Hatcher became mayor in 1968, the decline of industrial cities across the country had begun. The election of Hatcher—one of the nation's first big-city, African-American mayors—was hailed as a historic civil rights achievement, but it hastened the flight of white residents and businesses to the suburbs.

"The fatal flaw was that it was indeed a one-industry town," explained Stephen G. McShane, curator of the Calumet Regional Archives and history professor at Indiana University Northwest in Gary. "When Gary Works and the steel industry did well, so did Gary. When Gary Works and the steel industry suffered, so did Gary."

The decline of the steel industry did to Gary what the decline of the auto industry did to Marion, Anderson, and Kokomo. Employment at Gary Works dropped from 30,000 at its peak to 5,000 today. The tax base fell accordingly.

Twenty-first century Gary is known more for high unemployment, high crime, and failing schools than for jobs, parks, and education. But efforts are under way to diversify its economy and revitalize its civic institutions.

"It'll never be the same as it was of course," said McShane, "but there are promising developments."

Two recent examples underscore his optimism: A $174.1 million runway investment at the Gary airport is expected to draw new cargo traffic that should bring jobs and additional commercial development. A $28.2 million grant from the Northwest Indiana Regional Development Authority paid for a complete restoration of Marquette Park, including the 1920s bathhouse and entertainment pavilion, making it once again a tourist destination of choice. In 2014 the project received the Cook Cup for Outstanding Restoration from Indiana Landmarks.

Directions: Marquette Park is at 1 North Grand Boulevard, Gary.

INDIANA PIONEERED EUGENICS
WITH 1907 LAW

Long before Adolf Hitler espoused his ideas about a master race, Hoosier scientists advocated selective reproduction to improve the gene pool.

Indiana governor J. Frank Hanly signed the nation's first eugenics law in 1907. The measure mandated sterilization of certain "criminals, idiots, rapists and imbeciles" in state custody. Thirty states followed suit.

"Today they couch it as a pseudo-science, but that's not the way scientists saw it at the time," said Jason S. Lantzer, history professor and honors coordinator at Butler University. "It was cutting edge."

Derived from the Greek words "eu," meaning good, and "genos," meaning offspring, eugenics pursued two seemingly compatible goals: promoting reproduction by people of strong mind and body, while discouraging procreation among the criminally deviant and mentally ill.

Reputable people accepted the theory that genes bore the blame for society's ills. Speaking in 1879 to the Social Science Association of Indiana, Harriet M. Foster contended that mental retardation was inherited. The Board of State Charities, which oversaw prisons, mental hospitals, and orphans' homes, likewise traced poverty, crime, and mental illness to genetics.

In 1901 the Indiana General Assembly passed a bill that made unsupervised, feeble-minded women aged sixteen to forty-five wards of the state to prevent them from bearing children. In 1905 the legislature prohibited marriage licenses for imbeciles, epileptics, and those of unsound mind. The 1907 law authorized state institutions, in consultation with "a committee of experts," to perform vasectomies on inmates for whom procreation was deemed inadvisable.

Why was Indiana first? A Hoosier doctor, Harry Clay Sharp, pioneered the vasectomy as a safer, less painful alternative to castration. Sharp performed the operation on about 225 prisoners at the Indiana Reformatory in Jeffersonville before the state had a law allowing it. "The 1907 law is in some ways a reaction to Harry Sharp," Lantzer explained.

This marker was installed in 2007 to the west of the Indiana Statehouse to observe the centennial of the nation's first eugenics law.

Governor Thomas R. Marshall halted the sterilizations in 1909 because of concerns about their constitutionality. In 1921 Governor James P. Goodrich observed that the law was not being followed, so he pushed for a test case in the courts.

In a decision ahead of its time, the Indiana Supreme Court struck down the law as a violation of the Fourteenth Amendment's due process clause. The court said the law violated inmates' rights by not allowing them to cross examine the state's experts or to argue that the operation was inappropriate for their condition.

Eugenics sputtered along for the next several years. In 1927 the U.S. Supreme Court reviewed a Virginia law that authorized sterilization of inmates suffering from insanity, idiocy, and epilepsy, among other traits. The law had been written with procedural protections so it might pass constitutional muster. In upholding the law, Justice Oliver Wendell Holmes famously wrote, "Three generations of imbeciles are enough." The ruling in *Buck v. Bell* led to an immediate rise in forced sterilizations across the country, and prompted Indiana to write a new law with a guaranteed appeals process.

Eugenics lost favor in the 1940s and 1950s due to Nazi Germany's barbaric practices and the United States's increasing awareness of individual rights. By then an estimated 65,000 people had undergone sterilization nationwide with California most aggressive at 20,000; Indiana's 2,400 paled by comparison.

In the 1970s Governor Otis R. Bowen pushed for the repeal of all sterilization and restrictive marriage laws in Indiana, and the legislature obliged. The *Buck v. Bell* ruling has never been overturned.

Directions: The historical marker remembering the state's eugenics law is located between the Indiana Statehouse and the Indiana State Library at 140 North Senate Avenue, Indianapolis.

INDIANA AUTHORS ENJOYED BEST-SELLING REPUTATIONS

It's been called the golden age of Indiana literature. During the first half of the twentieth century, Hoosier authors dominated the fiction best-seller list, rivaling states with far more established literary traditions.

Meredith Nicholson penned *The House of a Thousand Candles* (1905), Theodore Dreiser wrote *An American Tragedy* (1925), and Booth Tarkington won Pulitzer prizes for *The Magnificent Ambersons* (1918) and *Alice Adams* (1921).

Other popular fiction writers of their day included Lew Wallace, Gene Stratton-Porter, George Ade, Lloyd Douglas, and Charles Major, to name just a few.

The prolific careers of these and so many other Hoosiers have prompted scholars to wonder: What made the land of cars and cornfields a literary mecca in the twentieth century?

"There is no magic answer," replied Howard H. Peckham in his 1950 *American Heritage* magazine article on the subject. Peckham theorized that several factors converged after the Civil War to promote a Hoosier writing tradition. Among them: diversity of citizens, both ethnically and socioeconomically; an appetite for reading nurtured by literary clubs, libraries, and local publishers; openness to new ideas; and familiarity with the rich literary heritage of New England.

Two analyses of best-seller lists, one by John Moriarty in 1949 and another by Steven J. Schmidt in 1990, reached the same conclusion. Indiana led the nation in the production of popular authors from 1900 to 1941. Using a point system for top ten fiction titles, Indiana ranked first, followed by New York, with Pennsylvania and Virginia third or fourth, depending on the study.

Nicholson, born in Crawfordsville and an Indianapolis resident from the age of five, often said the key to popularity was to stick close to home. Many Hoosier writers did.

Tarkington, an Indianapolis native, built his plots and settings around life in the Midwest. In *The Gentleman from Indiana* (1899), he made specific references to the Indiana landscape, skies, and weather.

Nicholson's early novel *Zelda Dameron* (1904) was set in Mariona,

Meredith Nicholson lived here when he wrote The House of a Thousand Candles. *Built in 1904, it is believed to have been the first Georgian/Colonial Revival style home in Indianapolis.*

a pseudonym for Indianapolis. *The House of a Thousand Candles* was based on a mysterious old mansion on Lake Maxinkuckee at Culver. Nicholson wrote the book while living at 1500 North Delaware Street in Indianapolis. Fittingly, the residence today is headquarters for Indiana Humanities, a not-for-profit organization promoting literary and cultural arts.

With the passing of the golden age authors, a new generation of Hoosier writers arose to take their place in the latter half of the twentieth century.

Jessamyn West from Vernon wrote two bestsellers with Indiana plots. *The Friendly Persuasion* (1945) was made into a successful film starring Gary Cooper, and tells the story of a Quaker family living in Indiana during the Civil War. *The Massacre at Fall Creek* (1975) was a fictionalized account of a real crime in which white settlers killed Native Americans on the frontier.

By the early 1970s, Kurt Vonnegut of Indianapolis "was one of the most famous living writers on earth," according to biographer William Rodney Allen. Best known of his fourteen novels was *Slaughterhouse-Five* (1969), which he based heavily on his experience as a prisoner of war in Dresden, Germany, during World War II.

Living Hoosier authors with multiple blockbusters to their names include Dan Wakefield of Indianapolis (*Going All The Way*, 1970); historic fiction writer James Alexander Thom of Bloomington (*Follow the River*, 1981); and John Green of Indianapolis (*The Fault in Our Stars*, 2012).

To commemorate the state's bicentennial, the Indiana State Library created a literary map featuring 200 Hoosier writers from the state's ninety-two counties. A digital copy of the map can be viewed at http://www.in.gov/library/files/1816-2016_Literary_map_of_Indiana.pdf.

Directions: The Meredith Nicholson House, headquarters of Indiana Humanities, is at 1500 North Delaware Street, Indianapolis.

INDIANAPOLIS 500 SYNONYMOUS WITH INDIANA

On May 30, 1911, forty gentlemen started their engines for the inaugural Indianapolis 500 Mile Race. Indiana has never been the same.

No single event is as closely associated with Hoosiers as is the Indianapolis 500, dubbed the Greatest Spectacle in Racing by a radio copywriter in 1955.

When automotive entrepreneur Carl G. Fisher first conceived of a speedway in the early 1900s, he had no idea what a spectacle it would become. His goal was to have a testing facility for new cars that would occasionally pit manufacturers against each other to compare speed, gas mileage, and the like. "He believed that success on the track would translate into showroom sales," explained Indianapolis 500 historian Donald Davidson.

Fisher and three partners formed a company, purchased farmland, and opened a two-and-a-half-mile track in 1909. When the original surface of crushed rock and tar cause multiple accidents, they redid the surface with 3.2 million bricks.

At first, the track sponsored three-day meets with numerous races, but those events did not prove popular. In 1911 the owners announced a new format: an all-day race of 500 miles, to be held annually on Memorial Day weekend with generous prize money.

That year Ray Harroun drove his Marmon Wasp to victory before an estimated 90,000 spectators. His average speed was seventy-four miles per hour. Notably, Harroun's car was the only one-seater. The other drivers had riding mechanics in the passenger seat, who manually pumped oil and turned their heads constantly to check for competitors.

In response to complaints his car might pose a safety hazard, Harroun had installed a mirror above the steering area—an automotive accessory that would soon be deemed indispensable on consumer automobiles.

From the beginning the 500 "attracted immense crowds, and soon people were coming from everywhere," wrote Jeanette C. Nolan in her 1943 history of Indianapolis, *Hoosier City*. "European visitors timed

The Borg-Warner Trophy, bearing a likeness of each Indianapolis 500 champion, was established in 1935. The Indianapolis Motor Speedway Hall of Fame Museum has the original; the race winner receives a smaller sterling-silver replica.

their tours to include the Memorial Day race in Indianapolis. The novelty of its appeal seemed never to wear off, for each year was different and more exciting; more spectators, more entrants, larger prizes, previous speed records shattered to bits."

Indeed, change has been constant since the first race. To increase safety, the board of the American Automobile Association, the first sanctioning body, mandated a formula limiting the size of the starting field based on track size. With a few exceptions, the lineup has been thirty-three cars ever since.

In 1927 Fisher and partners sold the track to an investor group headed by World War I flying ace Eddie Rickenbacker, himself a racecar driver. During World War II, the track deteriorated due to inactivity, and it was sold again in 1945 to Anton "Tony" Hulman, who repaved most of the surface, built new and improved grandstands, and increased the prize money.

In 1977 the famous start-of-race command, "Gentlemen, start your engines," was altered to "Lady and gentlemen" to reflect the entry of the first woman qualifier, Janet Guthrie.

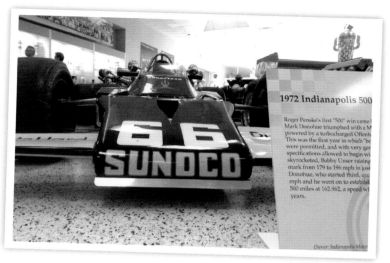

1972 Indianapolis 500

Roger Penske's first "500" win came
Mark Donohue triumphed with a M
powered by a turbocharged Offenh
This was the first year in which "b
were permitted, and with very go
specifications allowed to begin w
skyrocketed, Bobby Unser raising
mark from 179 to 196 mph in jus
Donohue, who started third, qu
mph and he went on to establis
500 miles at 162.962, a speed wl
years.

Owner: Indianapolis Moto

The Hall of Fame Museum's collection includes many cars that won the 500, including the Marmon Wasp driven by Ray Harroun in the 1911 race and this McLaren M-16B driven by Mark Donohue in 1972.

In the race's history, three drivers have won the Indianapolis 500 four times: A. J. Foyt, Al Unser, and Rick Mears. The fastest official lap recorded was 237.498 miles per hour by Arie Luyendyk during qualifying on May 12, 1996.

The Indianapolis Motor Speedway Hall of Fame Museum was established in 1956 to preserve the Speedway's history and honor IndyCar winners as well as leading figures from other motorsports, including the National Association for Stock Car Auto Racing and Grand Prix. The museum features trophies, goggles, race memorabilia, and dozens of historic racecars, including Harroun's Wasp with its original body manufactured by the Marmon Motor Car Company of Indianapolis.

Directions: The Indianapolis Motor Speedway and Hall of Fame Museum is at 4790 West Sixteenth Street in Indianapolis.

VICE PRESIDENT THOMAS MARSHALL PUT CONSTITUTION ABOVE SELF

For nearly a century, Indiana has been known as the Mother of Vice Presidents. Indeed, between 1868 and 1916, ten vice presidential nominees hailed from Indiana.

In 1916 Indiana could not miss: Thomas R. Marshall of Columbia City was running for re-election as Woodrow Wilson's vice president on the Democratic Party ticket, and Charles W. Fairbanks of Indianapolis was running as the Republican Party nominee on the ticket headed by Charles Evans Hughes. (Fairbanks had already served as vice president under Theodore Roosevelt from 1905 to 1909.) Wilson and Marshall won, with Marshall going on to complete a second full term.

Marshall was the only vice president born in Indiana until 1988, when Dan Quayle was elected as running mate to George H. W. Bush. Five lived in Indiana at the time of their election to the nation's second-highest office, second only to New York with eleven.

Indiana 9 between Marshall's home in Columbia City and Quayle's home in Huntington bears numerous signs declaring it the Highway of Vice-Presidents. The other Hoosier vice presidents were Schuyler Colfax Jr. from New Carlisle, who served with President Ulysses S. Grant from 1869 to 1873, and Thomas A. Hendricks from Shelbyville and Indianapolis, vice president with President Grover Cleveland from March 4, 1885, until Hendricks's death eight months later.

Marshall was born in North Manchester in 1854, spent much of his childhood in Pierceton, and attended Wabash College before studying law. He worked as an attorney in Whitley County from 1875 until becoming Indiana's governor in 1909. During his days as an attorney he lived in a two-story Italianate home in Columbia City. The Whitley County Historical Society was formed in 1958 to purchase his home, which is maintained as a county history museum. Curator Aaron Mathieu said that local residents have pitched in to restore Marshall's home to much of its original condition.

Mathieu pointed out that in 1919 Marshall was faced with a monumental decision no other American has faced or ever will. Wilson had suffered a debilitating stroke. Tremendous pressure was brought

The Whitley County Historical Museum maintains Thomas Marshall's home much like it would have looked in 1900.

to bear on Marshall to become the acting president. At the time, there was no process for him to do so. Fearing that he would precipitate a constitutional crisis, Marshall declined to assume the presidency. Wilson's cabinet and Marshall, with help from Wilson's wife, functioned as best they could without a formal transfer of power.

Did Marshall make the right decision? That question is still debated; even Marshall's detractors acknowledge that it took quite a man to step away from the opportunity to become president. Mathieu believes that Marshall's decision was in the finest American tradition of putting the Constitution above personal glory. In 1967 U.S. Senator Birch Bayh of Indiana shepherded the Twenty-fifth Amendment to the Constitution through ratification, establishing a constitutional process for transfer of power in the event a president is incapacitated.

Marshall was known for his self-deprecating wit. In his acceptance speech as vice president, he promised to "acknowledge the insignificant influence of the office." His best known saying, "What the country needs is a really good five-cent cigar," reflected his belief that the common man should be the focus of government policy.

Marshall died of a heart attack in 1927. He is buried in Crown Hill Cemetery in Indianapolis.

Directions: The Whitley County Historical Museum is at 148 West Jefferson Street in Columbia City.

STATE PARKS ARE ENDURING LEGACY FROM 1916 CENTENNIAL

In 1916 Indiana celebrated its one hundredth birthday with pageants, parades, and a presidential visit and gave the best gift imaginable to future generations of Hoosiers: a statewide parks system.

The planning began in 1915, when lawmakers created the Indiana Historical Commission (today the Indiana Historical Bureau) to oversee centennial events and to collect, edit, and publish materials related to Indiana history. The legislature appropriated $25,000 for the occasion.

Almost all of the state's ninety-two counties got into the act: Fayette County built a hospital and dubbed it Fayette Centennial Memorial, Jay and Carroll Counties put up new courthouses as centennial projects, and Tipton County raised money for a memorial fund to build a new auditorium.

Governor Samuel Ralston lobbied for better roads and convinced the general assembly to help fund Indiana's portion of the Dixie Highway, a north-south transcontinental route that, in part, followed today's US 31.

President Woodrow Wilson visited Indiana on October 12, declared by Ralston to be "Centennial Highway Day." Wilson delivered a lengthy address on the benefits of the Good Roads movement to a crowd of 7,000 at the Indiana State Fairgrounds Coliseum.

By far the most enduring legacy of the centennial was the establishment of the state parks system to "refresh and strengthen and renew tired people, and fit them for the common round of daily life," as explained by conservationist Richard Lieber, who had advocated land preservation since the early 1910s.

In something of a timely coincidence, the state was preparing for the centennial just as a pristine natural forest area in Parke County—a place called Turkey Run—was advertised for sale. The Hoosier Veneer Company of Indianapolis wanted to buy the land for its virgin timber.

By the time the property went up for public auction, the movement to establish a state park system had begun. Lieber had been named to the IHC, and the commission had established a parks committee. No tax dollars were available for land acquisition, so the

McCormick's Creek was Indiana's first state park, notable for its limestone canyon, flowing creek, and scenic waterfalls.

committee set about the task of raising money privately to buy Turkey Run.

In the meantime, Owen County citizens learned of plans by the estate of Frederick W. Denkewalter to sell McCormick's Creek Canyon, a limestone and wooded area with a flowing creek and scenic waterfall. The parks committee resolved to buy that land if Owen County residents chipped in one-fourth of the $5,250 price. They readily agreed.

"Thus, McCormick's Creek Canyon—and not Turkey Run—became the first link in the chain of parks established by the people of Indiana on the one hundredth anniversary of their statehood," observed Suellen M. Hoy, writing in the *Indiana Magazine of History*.

As for Turkey Run, Hoosier Veneer paid $30,200 for the property at auction, but bowed to pressure from the public and newspaper reporters and, in November 1916, sold it to the parks committee for a tidy $10,000 profit.

Lieber became nationally known for his role in the state parks movement and was named the first director of the Indiana Department of Conservation, today the Department of Natural Resources. The parks system rapidly expanded under his leadership. By 1930 there were nine parks with 479,000 visitors a year.

From the beginning, the parks charged an admission fee, initially ten cents, because of Lieber's insistence they be somewhat self-supporting. Today the standard daily entry fee is seven dollars for a carload of Hoosiers or fifty dollars for an annual pass. The DNR operates twenty-seven state parks, eight lakes, fourteen state forests, twenty-five fish and wildlife areas, and sixteen nature preserves.

Directions: McCormick's Creek State Park is two miles from Spencer, just off Indiana 46 at 250 McCormick's Creek Park Road.

HOOSIER FIRST AMERICAN TO DIE IN WORLD WAR I

Although few Hoosiers know his name, James Bethel Gresham of Evansville earned a place in the history books for his role in World War I.

Corporal Gresham of the First Division's Sixteenth Infantry was reportedly the first to die in the service of the American Expeditionary Forces.

A factory worker at the time of his enlistment in the U.S. Army, Gresham symbolized thousands of Hoosiers who were willing to give all for a cause not fully understood.

"He was an ordinary American, with no distinction of high birth, scholarship or social prestige," wrote Heiman Blatt in *Sons of Men: Evansville's War Record*, published in 1920. "Only an average American; yet, his name will be transmitted to posterity as the first American soldier who made the supreme sacrifice on the battlefield."

Indiana sent more than 130,000 soldiers to the Great War, and more than 3,000 died from battle wounds or disease. To this day, the reasons are hard to grasp. It began with a simple act of violence: the June 1914 assassination of Archduke Franz Ferdinand of Austria. It escalated into a global battle for dominance pitting the Central Powers (Germany, Austria-Hungary, Ottoman Empire, and Bulgaria) against the Allied Powers (Great Britain, France, Russia, and eventually the United States).

President Woodrow Wilson initially refused to get involved in the European war, sticking to a policy of isolationism or neutrality. After Germany violated a pledge not to wage submarine warfare in the North Atlantic, Wilson asked Congress for a war declaration in 1917.

Gresham was no novice when he arrived in Europe, having taken part in U.S. engagements in Mexico during the Mexican Revolution under the command of General John J. Pershing, the same general who would lead American forces in World War I.

Gresham's company had spent two months in Gondrecourt in northeastern France training in modern trench warfare before taking a position along the French line near Bathelmont.

According to a written account by Corporal Frank Coffman, the

Built in the 1920s to honor World War I veterans, the War Memorial has a neoclassical design that features a pyramidal dome and Ionic columns.

division had mostly retired for the night, "lured on by exhaustion and a sense of safety," when the Germans attacked in pitch dark on November 3.

In *The Doughboys: The Story of the AEF*, author Laurence Stallings described the scene: "Exactly at three o'clock in the morning all hell broke loose. Enemy guns spoke in chorus, tons of metal descended heavily along the Yanks' front, communicating trenches were plastered with mortar fire, machine guns sent their whispering streams of nickeled steel over the heads of the Doughboys in the line."

In the hand-to-hand combat, Gresham and Privates Thomas F. Enright and Merle D. Hay were killed, seven others were wounded, and eleven were taken prisoner. The deceased were buried on the battlefield, eulogized by a French general as "the first soldiers of the United States Republic to fall on the soil of France for justice and liberty."

The men were later reburied in the American Cemetery in Bathelmont. In 1921 Gresham's remains were returned to Evansville and interred in Locust Hill Cemetery.

In 1920 the Indiana General Assembly voted to construct the Indiana World War Memorial and Plaza to remember Hoosiers' involvement in the Great War, a mission eventually expanded to include subsequent wars as well. To the north of the memorial, a cenotaph dedicated to Gresham is surrounded by four columns topped by eagles. Fittingly, General Pershing came to Indianapolis to lay the cornerstone on July 4, 1927.

Directions: The Indiana War Memorial is at 431 North Meridian Street, Indianapolis.

EUGENE V. DEBS OPPOSED WAR CHAMPIONED LABOR

"The master class has always declared the wars; the subject class has always fought the battles. The master class has had all to gain and nothing to lose, while the subject class has had nothing to gain and all to lose, especially their lives."

With those words—and a few more like them—Hoosier socialist Eugene Victor Debs gave federal agents cause to arrest him for violating the Espionage Act in 1918.

The law, passed early in World War I, was meant to silence war protesters. It made it a crime to convey information "with intent to interfere with the operation or success of the military or naval forces of the United States or to promote the success of its enemies."

On the basis of his remarks at an antiwar rally in Canton, Ohio, Debs was tried, convicted, and sentenced to ten years in federal prison. Appealing to the U.S. Supreme Court, Debs unsuccessfully argued that the law violated his First Amendment right to free expression.

It was not the first time Debs drew national attention, nor would it be the last.

A lifelong Terre Haute resident, Debs was a labor organizer and five-time presidential candidate on the Socialist Party ticket. He played "a major role in popularizing socialism in America," wrote historian Clifton J. Phillips in *Indiana in Transition, 1880–1920*.

Born in 1855, Debs inherited his affinity for the poor and working class from his immigrant parents. At age fourteen he dropped out of high school to work, first as a sign painter in the rail yards and next as a fireman on the Terre Haute and Indianapolis Railroad. His observations of working conditions inspired him to become involved in labor organizing. In 1893 he founded the American Railway Union.

During its first year the union called for a strike against the Great Northern Railway Company, which had been cutting wages. Within eighteen days, the company gave in to almost all Debs's demands. The success prompted workers to join the union by the thousands.

In 1895 the Pullman Company, maker of sleeper and luxury rail cars, cut its labor force from 5,500 to 3,300 and reduced wages by 25 percent. When the Pullman workers struck, the railway union called on members to refuse to operate trains that used Pullman cars. This disrupted rail traffic nationwide.

A federal court issued an injunction declaring the boycott illegal, and President Grover Cleveland summoned troops to assist in crushing the strike. Debs was arrested and imprisoned for six months for violating the injunction.

While in jail, Debs concluded that labor needed a louder voice in the political system to push for change. By 1897 he declared himself a socialist, advocating government ownership of the means of production.

In March 1900 the Social Democratic Party held its first national convention in Indianapolis and tabbed Debs as its presidential candidate. He ran again in 1904, 1908, 1912, and 1920, the last while in prison on the espionage charge. Campaigning mostly by writing letters, Convict Number 9653 pulled in approximately 900,000 votes.

President Warren Harding commuted his sentence on Christmas Day 1921 in recognition that the law had been wrongly used to muffle him. Debs returned home to Terre Haute, where 50,000 citizens greeted him. He died in 1926.

The house where he spent much of his adulthood is now the Eugene Debs Museum. It contains many original pieces, personal effects, and historic photos. Designated a National Historic Landmark in 1966, the museum is open to the public five days a week.

Directions: The Eugene V. Debs Foundation office and museum are at 451 North Eighth Street, Terre Haute.

EVANSVILLE COURIER AND PRESS

Eugene Debs lived in this home with his wife Kate from 1890 until his death in 1926.

KLAN ENJOYED SHORT-LIVED POLITICAL POWER

During the 1920s, the Ku Klux Klan took Indiana by storm. Ninety years later, Hoosiers still struggle to grasp why.

The secretive brotherhood launched its Indiana recruitment efforts in Evansville in 1920. Within four years, Hoosier Klansmen numbered 250,000 and represented every corner of the state.

"Members included ministers, mayors, shopkeepers and factory workers, mostly ordinary people from the wide middle of society," noted historian James H. Madison in his book *Hoosiers: A New History of Indiana*. "These were mainstream Hoosiers, not a fringe group."

This was not the same Klan that arose after the Civil War in opposition to Reconstruction, the Republican program to bring opportunity and equal protection of law to newly freed slaves. The first Klan faded away in the 1870s after President Ulysses S. Grant persuaded Congress to pass legislation outlawing it as a terrorist group.

The second Klan emerged in the South at the turn of the twentieth century and rapidly expanded to Middle America. It proclaimed a message of patriotism, Prohibition enforcement, and Christian values. It preached exclusion, too—of immigrants, blacks, Jews, and especially Roman Catholics.

"Just why any individual joined the Klan remains uncertain," Madison said. "Some did it because it was the thing to do or because it provided networking, social activity and a sense of belonging." Others were true believers in a moral crusade.

Another factor in Indiana was the charismatic, intimidating leadership of a man named D. C. Stephenson. A Texas native who briefly flirted with socialism, Stephenson moved to Indiana around 1920 to take a job with a coal company, according to historical accounts. He unsuccessfully ran for the Democratic nomination for Congress in 1922 and then became heavily involved in Klan recruitment.

Rising quickly in the ranks, Stephenson moved to Indianapolis to assume the duties of Grand Dragon, a position he accepted publicly on July 4, 1923, at a Kokomo rally attended by 100,000 Klansmen and their families. A few months later, he broke away from the national organization to create a rival Klan group.

The 1876 jail building at the rear of the Hamilton County Museum of History once housed D. C. Stephenson and another notorious criminal, Charles Manson.

In Indianapolis, Stephenson sought to exert his influence on the affairs of state. Politicians of both parties joined the Klan, but the majority were Republicans looking to curry favor with a large voting bloc. In the 1924 elections, the Klan published lists of preferred candidates, noting their religious affiliations and positions on key issues.

Stephenson backed Republican Edward L. Jackson's successful candidacy for governor and attended Jackson's inaugural gala, where William M. Herschell of the *Indianapolis News* recited his poem, "Ain't God Good to Indiana?"

Despite its perceived influence, the Klan had little impact on laws passed in the 1925 session of the Indiana General Assembly. That March Stephenson was charged with the brutal assault and subsequent death of an Indianapolis woman, Madge Oberholtzer, who had accompanied him on a trip to Chicago.

The case was moved to Noblesville in Hamilton County because of concerns that Stephenson could not get a fair trial in Indianapolis. Before and during the trial, Stephenson lived at the Hamilton County Jail, which today is open to the public as a history museum.

On November 14, 1925, a jury convicted Stephenson of second-degree murder. He was sent to the Indiana State Prison, where he leaked damaging information about political activities that ruined the careers of Jackson, Indianapolis mayor John Duvall, and others.

The trial and aftermath discredited the Klan, which overnight lost members by the thousands and faded from view almost as quickly as it appeared. A third Klan formed in the 1960s to oppose civil rights for African Americans but gained a limited following.

Directions: The Hamilton County Museum of History is at 810 Conner Street in Noblesville.

CAR COMPANIES THRIVED IN INDIANA

Two decades after Elwood Haynes drove his horseless buggy down a Kokomo street, cars had become all the rage in Indiana.

"From the beginning, Hoosiers loved cars," historian James H. Madison wrote in *Hoosiers: A New History of Indiana*. They loved driving them, and they loved making them.

As of 1919 Indiana boasted 172 companies building cars or car parts in more than thirty cities and towns. The automotive belt included Kokomo, Marion, Anderson, New Castle, Muncie, South Bend, Fort Wayne, Auburn, and Indianapolis.

"Hoosiers loved cars so much because the auto industry put a lot of food on a lot of tables," noted Drew Van De Wielle, curator of collections at the Studebaker National Museum in South Bend.

By 1925 the Indiana Highway Commission reported that "horse-drawn traffic has almost disappeared from our main highways."

Whether for driving to work, church, or a Sunday spin in the country, cars were so effectively marketed that consumers started buying them on installment plans.

Several Hoosier models attracted a national following for their sleek lines, bright colors, and reliable engines. Among the more popular: Auburn, Cole, Cord, Duesenberg, Marmon, and Stutz. In 1909 Indiana ranked second only to Henry Ford's Michigan in the number of cars produced.

The most successful of the classic car makers was Studebaker Brothers, based in South Bend, which had been making carriages and wagons since 1868. In the mid-1880s it was the world's largest maker of horse-drawn equipment, with annual sales topping $2 million.

When the car came along at the turn of the twentieth century, the brothers wisely changed course, producing their first electric car in 1902 and gas-powered vehicles by 1904. In 1910 the company acquired the second largest carmaker in Detroit and the following year reorganized as Studebaker Corporation.

The Great Depression and two world wars affected Studebaker's sales and product lines, as they did all carmakers, but the company weathered the storms and continued to produce popular models into the 1950s, including the 1947 Starlight Coupe and the 1950 "Bullet

Visitors to the Studebaker National Museum can step back in time by posing at the wheel of this 1950 Studebaker "Bullet Nose."

Nose." In 1950 more than 343,000 cars and trucks rolled off its assembly lines, generating a $22.5 million profit.

The Auburn Automobile Company achieved similar prestige after a rocky launch in 1903. When entrepreneur E. L. Cord took over operations, he revived the company applying the philosophy, "novelty sells." He lowered prices, ordered eye-catching paint combinations, and added state-of-the art eight-cylinder engines.

In 1926 Cord acquired the failing Duesenberg Motor Company of Indianapolis, named for brothers Fred and August Duesenberg, German immigrants who had developed a reputation for expert engineering. Cord assigned Fred the job of designing a high-powered luxury car that would outclass everything else on the market. The Model J featured a 265 horsepower engine and reached speeds of 115 miles per hour.

A changing labor market and mastery of mass production by the Big Three Automakers—General Motors, Ford, and Chrysler—spelled the demise of the independent Hoosier-owned companies. Most went out of business during the Great Depression. Auburn ceased production in 1936; Studebaker hung on until 1966.

Fortunately for Hoosiers, the stories of these fabled car companies are thoroughly documented at the Studebaker museum and the Auburn Cord Duesenberg Automobile Museum in Auburn.

The Studebaker collection dates to the 1860s and includes presidential carriages built for Ulysses Grant, Benjamin Harrison, Abraham Lincoln, and William McKinley.

The Auburn museum, a National Historic Landmark, is housed in the building that served as the company's international headquarters from 1930 to 1936. It is considered an exceptional example of the art-deco style with its terrazzo floor lit by art-deco chandeliers and sconces.

Directions: The Studebaker National Museum is at 201 South Chapin Street, South Bend.

Directions: The Auburn Cord Duesenberg Automobile Museum is at 1600 South Wayne Street, Auburn.

The Gallery of Classics on the top floor of the Auburn Cord Duesenberg Museum features this 1936 Pierce-Arrow with its helmeted archer hood ornament.

VIRGINIA JENCKES WAS FIRST FEMALE HOOSIER IN CONGRESS

Riding President Franklin D. Roosevelt's coattails while declaring herself "my own boss," Democrat Virginia E. Jenckes unseated a sixteen-year incumbent in 1932 to become the first Indiana woman to serve in Congress.

A native of Terre Haute, Jenckes began her political career at age fifty-five after getting a taste of politics—and liking it—while lobbying for flood control in her hometown.

"Virginia Jenckes was quite a woman," noted Marylee Hagan, executive director of the Vigo County Historical Society and Museum, which maintains documents and photos of Jenckes in its archives.

Among her many achievements, Jenckes managed a farm, spearheaded a national campaign to make a navigable river corridor from Lake Erie to the Gulf of Mexico, and was the first woman to serve as a delegate to the International Parliamentary Union in Paris.

Born in 1877 to Mary and James Somes, Virginia attended public schools in Terre Haute and spent one year in college at the Indiana State Normal School. In 1912 she married a businessman thirty-four years her senior, Ray G. Jenckes, manager of the American Hominy Company mill in Terre Haute. The couple had a daughter and owned a 1,300-acre farm on the banks of the Wabash River.

When Ray Jenckes died in 1921, Virginia took over management of the farm and got involved in politics, becoming an officer in the Wabash-Maumee Improvement Association.

In 1932 Jenckes ran for the U.S. House of Representatives—a daunting task after the legislature redrew district boundaries to reflect population changes from the 1930 census. In order to win the seat, Jenckes had to beat two incumbents, first in the primary and then in the general election.

She succeeded, campaigning almost entirely on two issues: federally funded flood control and repeal of Prohibition, both which she said would help farmers in her district. Boosted by Roosevelt's landslide in the presidential race, Jenckes won the general election with 54 percent of the vote.

Although gender was rarely an issue for her, "not all went smoothly," noted Edward K. Spann in the *Indiana Magazine of History*. "On her

The image of Virginia Jenckes appears beneath the outstretched arms of labor organizer Eugene Debs in this mural by Bill Wolfe. It is one of four murals depicting the history of the Terre Haute area in the Vigo County Courthouse rotunda.

first day in the House of Representatives Jenckes provoked a minor crisis by wearing her favorite red hat, unwittingly violating a House rule against wearing hats."

Her congressional biography describes numerous achievements from her three terms in the House: "One of her first House votes was to support the Cullen Beer Bill— allowing for the production, transportation, and sale of the beverage—which passed by a wide margin in March 1933. She also managed to secure $18 million in funding during the following Congress for a series of flood control projects along the Wabash River Basin."

Like most Democrats, Jenckes supported New Deal legislation that established work relief, farm supports, public housing, and the Civilian Conservation Corps. She voted in 1935 for the Social Security Act, but when her time came to collect benefits she declined. "I think when you give dole to people you take away their self respect," she explained.

Growing discomfort with the scope of the New Deal cost Jenckes re-election in 1938 when she lost to Republican Noble Johnson.

In retirement, Jenckes gained national attention for helping five priests escape Hungary during a 1956 uprising. Late in life she returned to Terre Haute, where she died in 1975. Her likeness is included in a mural of fifty-two influential Vigo County citizens by artist Bill Wolfe prominently displayed in the Vigo County Courthouse rotunda.

Directions: The Vigo County Courthouse is at 33 South Third Street, Terre Haute.

PAUL McNUTT WIELDED UNPRECEDENTED POWER AS GOVERNOR

If Franklin D. Roosevelt had not run for an unprecedented third term in 1940, there is a good possibility that Hoosier Paul V. McNutt of Franklin would have become the thirty-third U.S. president.

One of the most powerful politicians Indiana has ever seen, McNutt had "astonishingly good looks," according to *Life* magazine. He displayed "a moment of destiny air," said *Time* magazine, which put him on its July 10, 1939, cover.

As it turned out, Roosevelt ran again, and destiny bypassed McNutt. An unusual coincidence was that the Republican Roosevelt beat for the presidency in 1944 was Wendell L. Willkie of Elwood, a good friend and fraternity brother of McNutt when they both attended Indiana University.

McNutt enjoyed a meteoric career. He graduated from IU and Harvard Law School, served in the U.S. Army in World War I, became the youngest dean in the history of the IU School of Law in 1925, and was selected to be national commander of the American Legion in 1928. Four years later, he became the first Democrat in twenty years to be elected governor of Indiana, and he went on to be an enthusiastic supporter of Roosevelt's New Deal.

The Indiana Constitution forbade McNutt from seeking a consecutive term as governor, and he never again ran for public office. In his one term, McNutt reorganized state government to centralize authority in the governor's office and used that authority to push through New Deal legislation and a major shift from property to income taxes.

Controversially, he established the Hoosier Democratic Club, called the "2 Percent Club," which encouraged state employees to pay that fraction of their salary to the Democratic Party to fund campaigns, thus allowing McNutt to amass political power that extended beyond his term as governor.

In 1937 Roosevelt named McNutt High Commissioner to the Philippines, a position he held until 1939, when he became head of the new Federal Security Agency, which oversaw a variety of New Deal programs.

The Indiana University campus in Bloomington displays two sculptures of Paul V. McNutt: a bronze head-and-shoulders bust in the Memorial Union between the two doors to Alumni Hall (above) and a marble one in the McNutt Residence Center (top).

While in the Philippines, McNutt performed a noteworthy humanitarian service. He persuaded the U.S. State Department to allow the entry into the Philippines of thousands of Jewish refugees from fascist régimes, although at this time the refugees could not legally enter the United States in large numbers. McNutt exhibited a less tolerant attitude in 1942 as chairman of the War Manpower Commission when he publicly urged "the extermination of the Japanese *in toto*."

Following the Japanese surrender in 1945, McNutt served again as High Commissioner to the Philippines and then as U.S. ambassador to the Philippines. He returned to the United States to practice law in New York and Washington, D.C.

McNutt died in New York City at age sixty-three and was buried in Arlington National Cemetery. A historical marker notes the location in Franklin of his birth home, which no longer stands. He is remembered at IU by sculptures, paintings, and Paul V. McNutt Quadrangle, a residence hall complex named for him.

Historian James H. Madison observed some time ago that "Paul McNutt towers over the 1930s, yet there exists no satisfactory biography." The omission was remedied in time for the state's bicentennial. In January 2015 Dean J. Kotlowski, professor of history at Salisbury University in Maryland, published *Paul V. McNutt and the Age of FDR*. This book, representing ten years of research and writing, is 428 pages with 108 pages of footnotes.

Directions: The Indiana Memorial Union is at 900 East Seventh Street in Bloomington. The McNutt Quadrangle is at 1101 North Fee Lane.

1937 OHIO RIVER FLOOD
SWAMPED EVANSVILLE

Even on the most beautiful of days, a walk along Evansville's River-front Esplanade evokes memories of the worst natural disaster in the history of the Ohio River—the Great Flood of 1937.

The levee is the most visible reminder, built by the U.S. Army Corps of Engineers to protect the city from a future catastrophe. For seventeen miles, earth embankments and concrete floodwalls serve as a border between the people of Vanderburgh County and the river.

There is a staff gauge on the pump house hash marked to fifty-four feet—the height at which the 1937 floodwaters finally stopped rising after twenty-two days above flood level.

There are literal signs, too. Along the landscaped river walk on top of the levee, historic markers tell the story of the Evansville region, paying special attention to the role of the river in community life and the mechanics of the new and improved levee system.

"For the people who experienced the flood, this was the most dramatic experience of their life, other than World War II," noted Indiana historian Robert L. Reid. "The rains started in December and they kept coming and they kept coming and they kept coming until, by the middle of January, the Ohio was above flood stage virtually everywhere."

The rain combined with sleet and snow to create a hazardous scene all along the Ohio River, from Pittsburgh to Cairo, Illinois. Water covered 70 percent of Louisville, 90 percent of Jeffersonville, and most of New Albany. The flood killed 385 people in all, left one million homeless, and caused $250 million in property damage ($3.4 billion in today's dollars), according to one National Weather Service estimate.

Evansville residents had dealt with floods before, in 1907, 1913, 1927, and 1933. But when they awakened on the morning of January 10, 1937, to a thick layer of ice on top of already soaked ground, they suspected this one might be worse. A week later, the heaviest rains fell, submerging more than half the city. On January 24 martial law was declared. On January 31 the river crested at 54.74 feet.

The fifty-four-foot hash mark on the pump house shows just how high the water rose during Evansville's Great Flood.

Amazingly, though Evansville was among the hardest hit, no one drowned in Vanderburgh County. For more than a month lives were on hold. Schools and businesses closed, travel stopped, and the Indiana National Guard patrolled the streets.

Once waters receded, residents faced a massive cleanup and repair period, similar to that of a war zone. There were muddy homes with buckled floors and ruined furniture, caved-in streets, broken levees, and debris and excess water everywhere.

Even when those who lived through it are gone, the 1937 flood is something Evansville will not likely forget. The photographs of a city underwater are just too extraordinary.

In 2012, to mark the flood's seventy-fifth anniversary, the Willard Library published a photographic history of the flood, *Over the Banks of the Ohio*. Among the most graphic images: men in business suits

A state historic marker along Evansville's riverfront describes the elaborate flood control plan and levee system put in place after the flood of 1937.

standing in thigh-high water, residents paddling through streets in rowboats, relief crews stationed on rooftops, and Bosse High School surrounded on all sides by rising water. In one picture at the intersection of Washington and Kentucky Avenues, the water almost reaches a theater's marquee.

In August 1937 Congress passed the Flood Protection Act to ensure nothing like the Great Flood would ever happen again. Evansville's $55 million project, begun in 1939 and not completed until 1994, features raised levees, twenty pumping stations, and a system of closeable gates and sandbag structures that automatically activate when the river reaches a level that prevents normal drainage.

Directions: A 1.5 mile walkable riverfront trail starts at Sunrise Park at the intersection of Waterworks Road and Riverside Drive and goes by the Evansville Museum of Art, History and Science, 411 Southeast Riverside Drive.

ERNIE PYLE BROUGHT WORLD WAR II HOME TO READERS

"Life is completely changed for thousands of American boys on this side of the earth. For at last they are in there fighting."

Hoosier war correspondent Ernie Pyle wrote those words on December 1, 1942, while on assignment with U.S. forces in Algiers.

The United States had entered World War II in December 1941 after the Japanese bombing of the American fleet at Pearl Harbor. Exactly one year later, Pyle witnessed the first battle action in northern Africa; his columns brought war's reality into 14 million homes via the pages of daily newspapers.

"You dig ditches for protection from bullets and from the chill north wind off the Mediterranean," wrote Pyle. "There are no more hot-water taps. There are no post exchanges where you can buy cigarettes. There are no movies."

This was the human side of a global conflict that changed the world—and Indiana.

More than 363,000 Hoosiers served in the armed forces during World War II, and more than 10,000 died. On the home front, Indiana dropped everything to support the war effort. Hoosier citizens purchased $3 billion in war bonds; manufacturers produced $3.2 billion in war goods, from Studebaker military trucks in South Bend to P-47 Thunderbolt fighter planes at Republic Aviation in Evansville.

At the start of the war, Indiana had two major military installations; by the end, thirty-one dotted the landscape, including ten ordnance plants, seven air bases, and five training camps.

As in all wars, the daily acts of heroism were what distinguished Hoosiers, and Pyle was no exception. His placement on the ground, eye-to-eye with fighting forces, changed the way journalists covered war and the way civilians saw it.

Born in 1900 on a farm near Dana, Pyle had enlisted in World War I but was still in training when the armistice was declared. He attended Indiana University, taking journalism classes and working for the *Indiana Daily Student*. He left IU just short of graduation in order to take his first newspaper job in La Porte. His next job was with the Scripps-Howard newspaper chain for which he would do his prize-winning war reporting.

The Friends of Ernie Pyle is a nonprofit organization that maintains Pyle's birth home and two Quonset huts displaying his World War II possessions, columns, and other memorabilia.

Like many of the GIs he covered, Pyle was killed while doing his job, hit by Japanese gunfire on April 18, 1945, on an island just west of Okinawa.

A draft of a column he was preparing for the war's conclusion was found in his pocket the day he died, and included a haunting description of war dead "scattered over the hillsides and in the ditches along the high rows of hedge throughout the world. . . . Dead men in such monstrous infinity that you come almost to hate them."

Pyle's life is remembered at the Ernie Pyle World War II Museum in Dana by the Friends of Ernie Pyle, a nonprofit organization that rescued his birth home from demolition in the mid 1970s and took ownership of the site from the state in 2011.

"His legacy is not just his writing," noted Stephen Key, executive director of the Hoosier State Press Association and a member of the site's board. "He told family members back home what their loved ones were experiencing. When you read his columns, you can almost see and hear and smell what was going on."

The museum is open to the public Friday, Saturday, and Sunday from May through Veterans Day. It is available year-round for group tours by appointment.

Directions: The Ernie Pyle World War II Museum is located in Dana on Indiana 71, one mile north of US 36 in Vermillion County.

HICKAM FIELD RECALLS FAMOUS HOOSIER AIRMAN

U.S. Army Air Corps lieutenant colonel Horace Meek Hickam of Spencer, Indiana, played a central role in establishing the U.S. Air Force as a separate branch of the armed forces, but his name did not come to world attention until December 7, 1941.

Hickam Air Force Base in Honolulu, named posthumously after Hickam, adjoined Pearl Harbor and served as America's primary air base in the South Pacific. A central part of the Japanese strategy on December 7 was to bomb and strafe Hickam so harshly that the planes there could not get off the ground to defend the American fleet at Pearl Harbor.

The Japanese strategy succeeded that day, although the U.S. flag remained aloft at Hickam at all times. In the end, Hickam served as the hub for America's Pacific aerial network forces that eventually destroyed Japanese air power.

Hickam was born in Spencer in 1885. His father, Willis Hickam, was a distinguished attorney, but Horace chose a military career. He graduated from West Point in 1908 and was commissioned a second lieutenant in the Eleventh Calvary. When the United States entered World War I, he was promoted to major and assigned to the aviation section of the U.S. Signal Corps, where he received pilot training.

Following the war, he was appointed chief of the information division offices of the Director of Air Services. In 1932 Hickam was

promoted to lieutenant colonel and given command of the Third Attack Group, based at Fort Crockett, Galveston, Texas. He testified in Washington, D.C., and spoke eloquently in favor of establishing the air force as a separate branch of the armed services.

Hickam continued to fly extensively and performed the first U.S. military night landings. He made frequent flights to Spencer to visit his family, landing in rural fields to the delight of local citizens.

A display at the Owen County Heritage and Cultural Center memorializes Spencer's native son, aviation pioneer Horace Hickam.

Hickam was tragically killed in a night landing at Fort Crockett, Texas, on November 5, 1934. He was buried at Arlington National Cemetery. Hickam Air Force Base (now Hickam Field) was named in his honor on May 21, 1935, and was activated in 1938.

Jessie Higa, historian of U.S. military and Hawaiian history in Honolulu, believes that the air force would not have been established as a separate branch of the military were it not for the advocacy and heroics of Hickam; and that Hickam would likely have been the first air force chief of staff but for his untimely death. She noted that his younger brothers went on to lead lives of distinction: Willis Jr. as an attorney in Spencer, and Hubert as one of the founding partners of the Indianapolis law firm Barnes and Thornburg.

As an active U.S. military installation, Hickam Field is not open to the public. The movie shown at the USS *Arizona* Memorial at Pearl Harbor reports extensively on the role of Hickam Air Force Base on December 7, and throughout the war.

The museum at the Owen County Heritage and Cultural Center houses a display in honor of Hickam. "The Hickam family was very prominent in Spencer," noted museum curator Vic Kinney. "Horace grew up on Main Street." The display features photos of Hickam's life in Spencer and highlights honors and promotions from his military career. The center is open to the public in the morning Tuesday through Friday.

Directions: The Owen County Heritage and Cultural Center is located at 110 East Market Street, Spencer.

USS *INDIANAPOLIS* PLAYED KEY ROLE IN WAR BEFORE TRAGIC END

The city of Indianapolis will be forever linked to one of the worst naval disasters in American history: the sinking of the USS *Indianapolis* in World War II.

A 10,000-ton, Portland class heavy cruiser, the *Indianapolis* delivered secret components for the atomic bomb to be used against Japan, only to be sunk by an enemy submarine's torpedoes on the return trip. More than 870 men died in shark-filled waters, and the ship's captain, Charles McVay III, was unjustly blamed in a court martial; his name was finally cleared long after he took his own life.

It is a story that deserved a better ending. The *Indianapolis* was the pride of the U.S. Navy, equipped with the latest technology and capable of traveling at thirty-two knots (more than thirty-six miles per hour). "Her speed and massive firepower truly captured the spirit of America," said Edgar Harrell, a survivor from Clarksville, Tennessee.

When the ship launched in 1931, its connection to Indianapolis was in name only. The U.S. Navy traditionally names cruisers after cities. In the years since, both Indianapolis and the survivors forged a meaningful relationship aimed at preserving the curiser's story.

On the eve of war, the ship's home port was Pearl Harbor in the Hawaiian Islands; luckily, on December 7, 1941, the *Indianapolis* was on a training mission at Johnston Island, located five hundred miles west of Hawaii. After the Japanese bombing of Pearl Harbor, the ship immediately joined the search for the attacking enemy carriers and remained in operation against the Japanese until its sinking.

Because of its reputation, the *Indianapolis* was selected by the navy in July 1945 to transport components for the atomic bomb used to destroy Hiroshima, nicknamed Little Boy. The ship did so with amazing speed, covering 5,000 miles from San Francisco to Tinian Island in the Pacific Ocean south of Japan in only ten days.

After the successful mission, the *Indianapolis* headed back to Leyte in the Philippines for training exercises in advance of an expected U.S. invasion of Japan.

The ship was halfway between the Philippines and Guam when a Japanese submarine, *I-58*, commanded by Mochitsura Hashimoto,

The memorial to the USS Indianapolis *tells the history of the cruiser on one side and lists the names of crew members on the other.*

spotted the cruiser. At 12:15 a.m. on July 30, two torpedoes struck the *Indianapolis*'s bow and starboard side.

Of 1,196 men on board, some three hundred went down with the ship. The rest jumped into pitch-dark water, infested with sharks, with only a few life rafts and almost no food or water. For reasons never made clear by the navy, the ship was not missed, and by the time the survivors were noticed by a pilot in the area four days later, only 316 men were alive.

The navy did not release the news to the press until August 15, the day Japan surrendered, no doubt to ensure the disaster would be overshadowed by joyous news.

Captain McVay survived the sinking, was court-martialed, and convicted of "hazarding his ship by failing to zigzag," a movement that could have evaded a torpedo strike. Evidence was overwhelming that the navy itself had placed the ship in harm's way, and that McVay was under no requirement to zigzag. Materials later declassified suggest the navy was trying to cover up its own culpability.

Thanks to relentless efforts of survivors and a 1996 National History Day project by Florida sixth grader Hunter Scott, both Congress and the the navy cleared McVay of wrongdoing in 2000 and 2001, respectively. Vindication came too late for McVay, who killed himself in 1968 using his navy-issued pistol.

Since 1960 survivors have routinely held reunions in Indianapolis to commemorate the crew's bravery. In 1995 the USS *Indianapolis* National Memorial was dedicated along the city's downtown canal. In 2007 the USS *Indianapolis* Museum opened as a gallery within the Indiana War Memorial.

Directions: The USS Indianapolis *Memorial is located at the north end of the Canal Walk (Walnut Street and Senate Avenue) in downtown Indianapolis. The Indiana War Memorial is at 431 North Meridian Street, Indianapolis.*

The War Memorial Museum displays memorabilia, photos and documents from all American wars and an extensive gallery devoted to the story of the USS Indianapolis.

BLACK COMMERCE AND JAZZ SIZZLED ON INDIANA AVENUE

In the segregated world of the twentieth century, a street called Indiana Avenue came to symbolize the identity and aspirations of Indianapolis's black citizens.

"It was the heart and soul of the African American community," said David Leander Williams, author of *Indianapolis Jazz*.

From the late 1800s, "the Avenue" offered a vibrant residential, commercial, and cultural environment for a growing black population. The middle class built homes there, entrepreneurs built businesses, and entertainers built a jazz reputation that rivaled Kansas City's and New York's.

Although its history is a source of pride, Indiana Avenue was a cultural nucleus by default rather than choice.

Early settlers had avoided the area because it was close to White River and believed to be a breeding ground for insects and disease. German and Irish immigrants and blacks moved there because it was all they could afford.

The first black-owned business opened on the Avenue in 1865, the year the Civil War ended. By 1870 close to 1,000 African Americans, a third of the city's black residents, lived there. By 1916 there were 142 homes, thirty-three restaurants, twenty-six grocery stores, sixteen clothing shops, and a medical practice started by a black physician, Doctor Joseph H. Ward.

Success breeds success, and Indiana Avenue was no exception. Madam C. J. Walker, born Sarah Breedlove in Louisiana in 1867, became one of the country's wealthiest women after developing a line of hair-care products including scalp ointment and hair soap. In 1910 she moved her business to Indianapolis because of the city's access to railroads and highways and Indiana Avenue's reputation as a good place for folks with enterprise.

The Madame C. J. Walker Manufacturing Company incorporated in Indiana in 1911. Walker lived in a house adjacent to her factory on West Street right off Indiana Avenue.

After Walker's death in 1919, her daughter took over the firm and oversaw an expansion that included construction of a new headquarters

PHOTO BY TOM BROGAN

Built in 1927 the Madame Walker Theatre Center is a National Historic Landmark and a notable example of African-inspired art deco architecture.

at 617 Indiana Avenue in 1927. The African-inspired building with terra cotta trim was the crown jewel of the neighborhood, housing not only the Walker offices and factory but also a community center with a 944-seat theater, ballroom, beauty shop, and drugstore.

During its first year, the theater hosted such black entertainers as blues queen Mamie Smith and Her Jazz Hounds and the Whitman Sisters. The Blackbirds, an orchestra led by Indianapolis pianist Reginald DuValle, was a local favorite.

Over the next two decades, Indiana Avenue enjoyed a golden age of jazz. More than twenty clubs did a lively business, attracting black and white audiences and frequent visits from big-name performers such as Louis Armstrong, Duke Ellington, Count Basie, Cab Calloway, Lionel Hampton, and Miles Davis.

Indiana Avenue created big names, too, among them trombone player J. J. Johnson, trumpeter Freddie Hubbard, guitarist Wes Montgomery, and saxophonist Alonzo "Pookie" Johnson, all Indianapolis natives.

The Avenue "was very much like a section of Harlem, with two or three major ballrooms and clubs dotted all the way from Ohio Street

The city's jazz heritage is depicted on the parking lot wall at Musicians' Repair and Sales, 332 North Capitol Avenue in Indianapolis.

and Indiana Avenue to Lockefield Gardens (a public housing project)," noted David Baker, an Indiana University professor, jazz composer, and virtuoso trombonist who started his career there. "It was the center of black culture, a place where music played six nights a week, all night long."

Today, few buildings from Indiana Avenue's past remain, most torn down to make way for newer developments such as the Indiana University–Purdue University at Indianapolis campus. The Madame Walker Theater Centre is the only remaining landmark, still serving as a cultural center, depository of black history, and performance venue.

Directions: The Madame Walker Theatre Center is at 617 Indiana Avenue in Indianapolis.

WENDELL WILLKIE RAN CREDIBLE RACE AGAINST FRANKLIN D. ROOSEVELT

Although many might be tempted to confer the honor on Benjamin Harrison, Wendell L. Willkie is the only native Hoosier ever nominated for president by a major political party. (Harrison was from North Bend, Ohio.)

Born and raised in Elwood, Willkie was the Republican standard-bearer in 1940, securing the nomination on the sixth ballot at the party's national convention. As of the first ballot, Willkie was in third place behind Thomas Dewey and Robert Taft; loud shouts of "We want Willkie" from the gallery helped turn the tide in what is considered one of the most exciting conventions ever.

Willkie gave Franklin D. Roosevelt his closest race yet, drawing 22.3 million votes. This was more than any GOP presidential candidate had ever received, and 5.6 million more than Alf Landon garnered for the Republican Party in 1936. However, the country was not ready to change leadership with Adolf Hitler menacing Europe, and voters returned Roosevelt to office for an unprecedented third term with 27.2 million votes.

Prior to 1940, Willkie enjoyed a distinguished career as a lawyer and politician. He was a civil rights activist and a leading critic of isolationism. In 1943 he published a book of his world travels titled *One World*, which spent four months atop *The New York Times* best-seller list. In his book, Willkie argued forcefully that the United States could not isolate itself from the rest of the world if it wanted a peaceful future.

Willkie died in August 1944 following a heart attack. He was the last nominee of either major party never to have held elected or appointed office.

According to Elwood resident and former Tipton mayor Dave Berkemeier, whose grandfather operated a farm owned by Willkie, "It was a great day for Elwood when Willkie accepted the Republican nomination. Over 250,000 people crammed into Elwood's Callaway Park to hear his acceptance speech."

Berkemeier and Elwood Chamber of Commerce executive director Marcy Fry both lamented that there is little left in Willkie's hometown

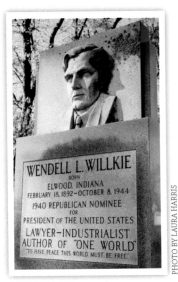

Wendell Willkie Park features this monument to the 1940 presidential candidate.

of about 8,500 people to commemorate its illustrious citizen. "There is not even a street named after him or a sign at the town entrance," said Fry.

The local high school was named Wendell L. Willkie High School, but after it burned to the ground in 1988 the new high school was simply named Elwood Community High School. Two of Willkie's former Elwood homes are still standing, but neither bears any Willkie designation. A small Wendell L. Willkie Park, two archways, and two plaques at Callaway Park are the primary remembrances in Elwood of Willkie today.

Fry suggested that Willkie's relationship with Elwood frayed when he failed to carry either Elwood or Madison County in the 1940 election. These were historically Democratic areas, which perhaps did not look kindly on Willkie's switching allegiance from the Democratic Party to the Republican Party in the late 1930s based on his belief that large federal projects such as the Tennessee Valley Authority infringed on the private enterprise system. Willkie was reportedly angry that his county did not show him more loyalty and spent most of the rest of his life on a farm he owned in his wife's hometown of Rushville, where he is buried at East Hill Cemetery. The largest public collection of Willkie memorabilia is in the Rush County Historical Society Museum, located at 619 North Perkins Street in Rushville.

Directions: Wendell Willkie Park, a memorial to the unsuccessful presidential nominee, is at the intersection of Indiana 13 and North E Street. Callaway Park, where Willkie accepted the presidential nomination, is at 1135 North Nineteenth Street in Elwood.

SHERMAN MINTON AND *BROWN V. BOARD OF EDUCATION*

Chief Justice Earl Warren gets most of the credit, and rightly so, for the 1954 U.S. Supreme Court decision in *Brown v. Board of Education* outlawing segregated schools. But were it not for a Hoosier—Justice Sherman Minton of Floyd County—the *Brown* case would not have even been before the Court at that time.

In 1952, prior to Warren's appointment, the Court had to decide whether or not to take the case. The majority was against it, including Chief Justice Fred Vinson. However, only four "yes" votes are needed to hear Supreme Court appeals. Minton provided one of those votes, along with Justices William O. Douglas, Harold Burton, and Hugo Black.

According to Linda C. Gugin, coauthor of *Sherman Minton—New Deal Senator, Cold War Justice,* Minton's position in *Brown* "was very consistent with his progressive views on civil rights."

Minton expressed discomfort with racial discrimination in his highly regarded 1953 opinion in *Barrows v. Jackson*. The case involved a covenant in a deed that barred the sale of a residence to a non-white. As stated by Minton: "The question we now have is: can such a restrictive covenant be enforced at law by a suit for damages against a co-covenanter who allegedly broke the covenant?" Minton's answer was a resounding "no."

In the *Brown* case a year later, Minton played a key role in encouraging a unanimous court. He later called it "the most important decision of the century because of its impact on our whole way of life."

Born in Georgetown in 1890, Minton attended New Albany High School and earned a law degree from Indiana University in 1915. He was elected as a Democrat to the U.S. Senate, serving from 1934 to 1941, and was a strong supporter of President Franklin D. Roosevelt, including Roosevelt's plan to pack the Supreme Court by adding justices who would support New Deal legislation. Minton lost his bid for re-election.

His friend and former Senate colleague Harry S Truman appointed Minton to the Supreme Court in 1949, where he served until 1956, retiring due to steadily worsening anemia. He returned to New Albany, served occasionally as a judge on lower federal courts, and gave

PHOTO BY LAURA HARRIS

Shortly after Justice Minton's retirement from the Supreme Court in 1956, Governor George N. Craig commissioned his bust to be placed on display at the Indiana Statehouse.

speeches and college lectures. Minton died in 1965. He was the last member of Congress to be appointed to the Supreme Court.

Minton was considered to be in the conservative wing of the court, arguing for judicial restraint and opposing "legislating from the bench." Some commentators felt he became more conservative than he had been when he was an enthusiastic New Deal supporter. Gugin believes that he was consistent in his populist view that the court should not usurp the will of the people as expressed by elected representatives.

Minton is often referred to as Indiana's only Supreme Court Justice, but that is not the case. Willis Van Devanter, who served on the court from 1911 until 1937, was born and raised in Marion.

In Minton's memory, an elegant bust by Robert Merrell Gage is displayed in the Indiana Statehouse Rotunda. The Sherman Minton Bridge spans the Ohio River between Indiana and Kentucky, and the Minton-Capehart building houses federal offices in downtown Indianapolis. A plaque marks the house where he was born in Georgetown.

Directions: The Indiana Statehouse is at 200 West Washington Street, Indianapolis.

FORT WAYNE: A CITY OF ENTREPRENEURS

A wave of high-tech creativity in the late nineteenth and early twentieth centuries cemented Fort Wayne's reputation as the Silicon Valley of its day.

Some innovation highlights:

- Jenney Arc Lights illuminated League Park in Fort Wayne in 1883 for one of the earliest baseball games played at night.
- A self-measuring pump mechanism, devised in 1885 by Sylvanus Bowser, paved the way for today's do-it-yourself gas pumps.
- The 1921 Horton electric washing machine freed generations of housewives from the drudgery of washboards and hand-cranked wringers.

"Allen County has long been an internationally valuable center for innovation and entrepreneurship," said Todd Pelfrey, executive director of the Fort Wayne History Center.

The most famous entrepreneur with a Fort Wayne tie was Philo T. Farnsworth—an innovator in television-tube technology—who began the mass production of television sets in a Fort Wayne factory in 1939.

In Pelfrey's view, "Fort Wayne's most important twentieth century contribution to the international economy" was magnet wire. For a period in the 1910s and 1920s, Dudlo Manufacturing Company was the largest magnet-wire manufacturer in the country.

Magnet wire is a strand of copper or aluminum that, when coiled and energized by an electrical power source, creates an electromagnetic field. Electricity is useless without it, as George Jacobs understood when he started tinkering in his backyard shed.

The insulation is the key to the product's safety and efficiency, but until Jacobs's discovery the wire was typically insulated with cotton, which was bulky and subject to rapid wear and tear.

Jacobs, a native of Dudley, Massachusetts who worked in the paint business, created an enamel insulation with high-flash naphtha and tung oil, among other ingredients, which created a consistent coating on the finest of wire. He began producing the mixture on a limited scale and called his new business Dudlo, combining the words Dudley and Ohio, where he and his wife lived at the time.

A side-by-side comparison of the 1920 and 1950 models shows the progression of the automatic clothes washer made by Horton Manufacturing Company of Fort Wayne.

Lured to Fort Wayne by the promise of an investment from his father-in-law, Jacobs built a small plant, located on Wall Street, where he and a few employees began producing magnet wire full time. The business expanded rapidly to accommodate demand from radio and telephone makers and from Ford Motor Company, which was seeking huge amounts of small insulated wire for ignition assemblies.

At its peak the business operated around the clock and employed 6,000 workers from Fort Wayne and nearby communities. In its twenty-six-year existence, the company produced an estimated 35 million pounds of enameled wire, according to the 1965 history of the Dudlo Manufacturing Company by Roy Bates and Kenneth Keller.

In 1927, with economic uncertainty on the horizon, Jacobs sold the company to General Cable Corporation; his superintendent, Victor Rea, stayed on to manage the plant.

The presence of magnet-wire makers had a ripple effect on the Fort Wayne economy. Magnavox, maker of radios, record players, and television sets, moved to Fort Wayne in 1931 to be closer to the industry so essential to its products. Company documents made note of Fort Wayne's "fine climate of invention." (Magnavox closed its Fort Wayne facility in 1975.)

Despite a series of sales, mergers, and acquisitions over the years, two magnet-wire manufacturers still operate in Fort Wayne: Rea Magnet Wire and Superior Essex.

The History Center features a permanent display called Allen County Innovation, with examples of many other Hoosier creations, including those of present-day entrepreneurs: Vera Bradley, designer of quilted cotton luggage and handbags; Fort Wayne Metals, maker of medical-grade wire; and Sweetwater Sound, nationwide dealer in digital recording systems.

Directions: The History Center is at 302 East Berry Street in Fort Wayne.

LOVE AFFAIR WITH CARS LED TO DRIVE-INS

For a trip back to the "good ol' days," nothing beats a burger at The Suds in Greenwood, where cruising, carhops, and curb service are still the main ingredients of a Saturday night on the town.

A uniquely American institution that developed along with car culture, the drive-in restaurant was introduced in the 1920s, enjoyed its heyday in the 1950s, and conceded victory in the 1970s to the more efficient drive-through restaurants symbolized by McDonald's and its golden arches.

Both trace their ancestry to Texas, where two businessmen opened a joint called the Pig Stand along the Dallas-Fort Worth Highway in 1921. Servers called "tray boys" delivered barbecued pork sandwiches and sodas to customers sitting in their cars.

The first Hoosier drive-in opened in West Lafayette in 1929. The Triple XXX was a franchise operation that served an acclaimed root-beer brand brewed at an Anheuser Busch facility in Galveston, Texas.

Root beer, burgers, and fried pork tenderloins were standard menu items at Indiana drive-ins. Popular chains included A&W and Dog n Suds, which claimed to have the "world's creamiest" root beer recipe.

Most early drive-ins were housed in undistinguished, boxy buildings that could be built almost overnight. Over time they evolved into eye-catching structures surrounded by parking lots with overhangs to shelter cars from the elements. Architecture to complement the drive-in's theme was a common marketing ploy. One example was the Wigwam in Indianapolis, later renamed the Tee Pee, a sprawling white building adjacent to the Indiana State Fairgrounds topped by a conical tepee structure resembling an American Plains Indian's home.

Perhaps the most distinguishing feature of the drive-in restaurant was the carhop, the name given to the waiters and waitresses who took orders and delivered the food on trays that clipped to the car window. The term was coined at the Pig Stand, where male servers competed for customers by hopping on to the car's running board as it drove up to the stand.

In 1948 Harry Snyder opened the first In-N-Out Burger in California, a drive-through hamburger stand that became the forerunner of the successful model used by McDonald's, Burger King, and other fast-food franchises. This doomed the drive-in, which "could not compete

Carhops still take your order at The Suds in Greenwood, open limited week-end hours in warm weather months. The drive-in began in 1957 under the name Dog n Suds.

with these new fast food, self-serve, low-cost chains," according to the *Encyclopedia of Food and Drink in American History*.

A notable exception is the SONIC chain, founded in the 1950s and based in Oklahoma City, with more than 3,500 restaurants that still rely on carhops, sometimes wearing roller skates. A handful of mom-and-pop drive-ins also continue to thrive, patronized by customers on nostalgic road trips.

At one time, there were more than 100 Triple XXX "thirst stations" in the United States and Canada. Only the Indiana restaurant and one in Issaquah, Washington, survived. Today the Triple XXX Family Restaurant, open year round but no longer offering curb service, is a favorite hangout for students at Purdue University.

The Suds in Greenwood, which opened as Dog n Suds in 1957, closed and reopened many times through the years until car enthusiasts stepped in to save it. The restaurant hosts a classic car show every Saturday night in warm-weather months that jams the parking lot and adjoining street.

"If you look up the word profit in the dictionary, you won't see The Suds," joked co-owner John Wagner. "It holds its own, which is fine with us. We do it for the nostalgia. There's still a lot of fun in it. And a lot of friendship."

Directions: The Suds is at 350 Market Plaza in Greenwood.

HOAGY AND COLE TOPPED THE SONG CHARTS

Two of the twentieth century's most popular songwriters hailed from Indiana, both so distinctive that the mention of their names brings to mind such familiar melodies as "Night and Day," "It's De-Lovely," "Georgia on My Mind," and "Stardust."

Cole Porter and Hoagy Carmichael grew up on different sides of the track but followed similar paths to celebrity.

Porter, born in Peru in 1891, had a privileged childhood as the grandson of one of Indiana's richest businessmen. With his family's encouragement, he studied violin and piano before he turned eight. By age ten, he had composed "The Bobolink Waltz," which his mother liked so much she paid to get it published.

Porter received an elite education, attending Yale University, where he wrote musical comedies and sang solos for the Glee Club. At his grandfather's insistence, he enrolled at Harvard Law School, but the dean suggested he transfer to the music program. He did. By 1930 Porter was living in New York City writing hit songs and scores for Broadway's most popular shows, including *Anything Goes* and *Jubilee*.

In 1937 Porter was seriously injured in a horse-riding accident that led to thirty operations and the eventual loss of his right leg. Although his physical disability ended his social life, it did not affect his genius. In 1948 he collaborated with writers Bella and Sam Spewack to create his Broadway masterpiece, *Kiss Me Kate*.

"Stardust" was the masterpiece that defined Carmichael, who, like Porter, showed musical talent at an early age. Born in Bloomington in 1899, Carmichael vowed to have a more comfortable life than his parents. His father was an electrician who struggled to make ends meet. His mother supplemented the family's income by playing the piano at fraternity dances at Indiana University and at silent movies. Hoagy learned to play the piano at her knee.

Carmichael attended IU for undergraduate and law school and, along the way, organized a jazz band and wrote songs. After graduating, he moved to Florida to fulfill his ambition of a law career, inking "Stardust" on the front pages of a book while waiting for business. When Carmichael unexpectedly heard a recording of one of his earlier pieces, "Washboard Blues," by Red Nichols and His Five Pennies, he decided to give up law for music.

Guests enjoy "It's De-Lovely" and other familiar tunes in the Cole Porter Room at the Indiana History Center.

Carmichael moved to New York City, where he met such greats as Louis Armstrong, the Dorsey Bothers, and a would-be songwriter by the name of Johnny Mercer. Carmichael and Mercer enjoyed a fruitful partnership; one of their earliest collaborations was "Lazy Bones," which became a sensation in 1933 at the height of the Great Depression.

Although Carmichael had fifty hit songs, nothing compared to "Stardust" in popularity or royalties. Carmichael wrote the song for instruments only; it rose to the top of the charts after lyrics were added by Mitchell Parish and is believed to be the most-recorded song of all time.

Porter died in 1964 and was extolled in his Associated Press obituary for "such an individuality of style that a genre known as 'the Cole Porter song' became recognized." Carmichael died in 1981, remembered by biographer John E. Hasse for his "strong and distinctive melodies" and a singing voice "as unmistakable as his nickname Hoagy."

The Eugene and Marilyn Glick Indiana History Center in Indianapolis, the home of the Indiana Historical Society, has a room dedicated to Porter's legacy that is a must-visit for his fans. An interpreter sings his biggest hits in the 1940s-style cabaret with digital piano, photographs, and videos about Porter's life. The Center's restaurant, in tribute to Carmichael, is called the Stardust Terrace Café.

Directions: The Eugene and Marilyn Glick Indiana History Center is at 450 West Ohio Street, Indianapolis.

COLUMBUS KNOWN FOR ENGINES AND AESTHETICS

Diesel engines made Columbus, Indiana, a Fortune 500 city. World-famous architecture put Columbus on the map. Give J. Irwin Miller credit for both achievements.

As chairman and CEO of Cummins Inc. from 1934 to 1977, Miller turned an unprofitable Indiana-based business into a global leader in diesel engines and related technology that today reports net income of $1.65 billion a year.

As a philanthropist and man of faith, Miller took seriously his company's obligation to improve its community. He founded the Cummins Foundation in 1954 to support worthwhile projects in his city and later to promote good causes in places where Cummins did business.

His most visible legacy was the architecture program, a public-private partnership through which the foundation funded design fees of public buildings—if they were designed by leading architects.

Thanks to that investment, Columbus (population 45,000) has seventy buildings and artworks by such masters as I. M. Pei, Eliel Saarinen, Eero Saarinen, Richard Meier, Harry Weese, Dale Chihuly, and Henry Moore.

"This is a pilgrimage place," said architect Will Bruder of Phoenix, who visited Columbus in 2012 for an American Institute of Architects conference on design excellence.

Miller's idea grew out of a building project that took place at his own church in the early 1940s. The First Christian Church had outgrown its space and wanted a new structure that was untraditional. The building committee approached Saarinen, a native of Finland known for his work at the Cranbrook Institute of Architecture and Design in Michigan.

Initially, Saarinen turned down the offer; a personal appeal by Miller persuaded him that the congregation was open to something radically different. Completed in 1942, it was the first contemporary building in Columbus and one of the first modern churches in the United States.

Eliel Saarinen's First Christian Church (1942) as viewed through Henry Moore's Large Arch sculpture that stands in Library Plaza.

In the 1950s Saarinen's son, Eero, famous for the Saint Louis Gateway Arch, designed three radically different structures for the Miller family: a vacation home in Canada, the Irwin Union Bank and Trust, and the Miller residence. The latter was notable because of its collaboration between Saarinen and interior designer Alexander Girard and landscape architect Dan Kiley

The public-architecture initiative was prompted by the post-World War II baby boom that necessitated new schools. Hoping to discourage bland institutional architecture that characterized typical school buildings, Miller proposed a novel relationship with the school board. His foundation would pay for the design of Schmitt Elementary if the school corporation would pay for construction. The results delighted everyone, and the program expanded to cover other public buildings, landscape, and streetscape projects.

Even the county jail was built with livability and aesthetics in mind. Designed by Don Hisaka in 1990, it is made of brick and Indiana limestone—complementing the nearby courthouse—with a recreation area covered by a wire-mesh dome.

Seventy-five years after Miller lured the Saarinens to town, Columbus remains committed to his vision. The Mill Race Center, offering senior services, is a recent example. Completed in 2011, the curving brick design by William Rawn Associates of Boston takes advantage of natural lighting with views of an adjacent city park.

The Columbus Area Visitors Center offers a variety of tours of Columbus's architectural landmarks, including the Miller home and gardens, which were donated to the Indianapolis Museum of Art by the family.

Directions: The Columbus Area Visitors Center, starting point for architecture tours, is at 506 Fifth Street in downtown Columbus. The First Christian Church is at 531 Fifth Street.

A COMMON IDENTITY BUILT UPON BASKETBALL

For the better part of Indiana's history, high school basketball has been the glue that binds citizens together.

Is there a Hoosier living who has not played the game, cheered at a sectional game, or seen the classic movie *Hoosiers* multiple times? Or has been inspired by the stories of the "mighty men of Milan" of 1954 or the Crispus Attucks Tigers of 1955?

"Early on I just couldn't understand why people were so passionate about high school basketball," broadcasting legend Tom Carnegie said in a 2010 interview for the hundredth anniversary of the Indiana high school basketball tournament.

Carnegie, a native of Connecticut, figured it out fast. "It was the topic of conversation everywhere—in the smallest burg in the state, in the biggest high school—and I think it was because they were all shooting for one big trophy, and that was the state championship," he said.

Indiana did not originate basketball, of course, but it sure welcomed it with open arms. James Naismith is credited with creating the game in 1891 in a Massachusetts Young Men's Christian Association to keep restless college men active in the winter.

Naismith nailed peach baskets to the lower rail of a gymnasium balcony, one at each end, and "basket ball" was born. His rules were printed in a magazine sent to YMCAs around the country, and the game spread like wildfire.

How and when it came to Indiana is unclear. Most Indiana basketball histories say that Reverend Nicholas McCay introduced the game at the Crawfordsville YMCA in the spring of 1893, with the first competitive game in March 1884 between teams from Crawfordsville and Lafayette.

More recent scholarship, however, suggests games had already been played elsewhere, including Indianapolis and Connersville. S. Chandler Lighty searched recently digitized late-nineteenth-century Indiana newspapers for references to basketball and found quite a few. He summarized his conclusions in an article for the *Indiana Magazine of History* : "Evansville seems to have been the site of the earliest competitive (non-exhibition) basketball games in the state."

Basketball teams in search of inspiration can rent out the Hoosier Gym for practice. The old Knightstown gym served as home court for the Hickory Huskers in the 1986 movie Hoosiers.

Regardless of its arrival date, basketball and Indiana was a match made in heaven. Hoosier farm boys could play it in the winter because it did not interfere with planting or harvest season. Urban youngsters could play it in a park. From the beginning, girls played too, although their tournament opportunities were limited until the gender equity movement of the 1970s.

The first boys high school state tournament was in 1911, Crawfordsville beating Lebanon 24–17. After that "the high school tournament became an annual rite, a sacred institution, a touchstone of Indiana culture," wrote William Gildea in *Where the Game Matters Most*, a study of the final season before the tournament switched from a single-class to multiclass format in 1997.

Two shining moments stand out in Hoosiers' collective tournament memory. One was the last-second, fourteen-footer by Bobby Plump in 1954 that lifted small-town Milan over powerhouse Muncie Central 32–30, a David versus Goliath story fictionalized in the movie *Hoosiers* and filmed in Indiana.

The first basketballs were meant to be thrown, not dribbled. This ball, used in 1910 at Beaver Dam High School in Akron, is the oldest in the Indiana Basketball Hall of Fame's collection.

The second occurred the very next year, when Oscar Robertson led the Crispus Attucks Tigers to the state championship, becoming the first all-black team to win the state title—a feat repeated by Attucks in 1956 in the face of widespread racial prejudice encountered on opponents' courts.

Those stories and much more are memorialized at the Indiana Basketball Hall of Fame in New Castle. Its 14,000-square-foot museum documents the teams, players, and coaches behind Hoosier Hysteria from the 1890s to the present.

Directions: The Indiana Basketball Hall of Fame is at 408 Trojan Lane, New Castle.

Directions: The Hoosier Gym is at 355 North Washington Street, Knightstown.

PURDUE ASTRONAUTS BRAVED THE FINAL FRONTIER

Before they were superheroes of the Space Age, they were students at Purdue University.

Virgil "Gus" Grissom, a native of Mitchell in Spencer County, Purdue class of 1950, was one of seven original astronauts selected by the National Aeronautics and Space Administration for Project Mercury, the United States' first man-in-space program.

Roger Chaffee, Purdue class of 1957, helped develop flight-control communications and instrumentation systems for the Apollo program.

Neil Armstrong, Purdue class of 1955, served as spacecraft commander for *Apollo 11*, the first manned lunar landing mission.

Eugene Cernan, Purdue class of 1956, flew to the moon twice. As commander of *Apollo 17* in 1972, he was the last man to have left his footprints there.

"The word astronaut was not common in the English language in the early 1950s when these guys were all on campus," noted aviation historian John Norberg, who has written and spoken extensively about Purdue's alumni astronauts. "It was an obscure word in science fiction then."

But it wasn't obscure for long, thanks in large part to Purdue's role—second only to the Massachusetts Institute of Technology—in educating astronauts for NASA.

Consider these facts:

- Purdue alumni have flown on 37 percent of all human U.S. space flights.
- More than forty space shuttle flights have had Purdue alumni on board.
- Two Purdue grads, including Indianapolis native David A. Wolf, were among the six American astronauts who have served on board *Mir*, the Russian space station.

By far the most famous Purdue astronauts have been Grissom and Armstrong, Grissom because of his pioneering achievements and tragic death during testing of the *Apollo 1* spacecraft, and Armstrong because he was the first man to walk on the moon.

Visitors to the Gus Grissom Memorial can see up close the Gemini 3 *two-man spacecraft that carried Grissom and John Young into space on March 23, 1965.*

As part of Project Mercury in 1961, Grissom piloted the *Liberty Bell 7* spacecraft on a fifteen-minute suborbital flight, becoming the second American in space. Four years later, he made history at the helm of *Gemini 3*, which flew nearly 81,000 miles and completed three orbits of the earth with crewmate John Young.

Dubbed the coolest heads in the business, Grissom, Chaffee, and Edward White were picked for the first mission of the Apollo spacecraft—the machine designed to send men to the moon. Disaster intervened on January 27, 1967, when a flash fire broke out inside the command module during a ground test; all three astronauts were killed. They were the first fatalities of the U.S. space program.

An irony of the tragedy was that it expedited the triumph of the Apollo program. "Because the accident happened on the ground, instead of in space, investigators could determine what areas needed the most attention to ensure the success of future missions," observed Grissom biographer Ray E. Boomhower.

To memorialize Indiana's hero, the Indiana General Assembly established the Virgil I. Grissom Memorial and Museum at Spring Mill State Park near Grissom's hometown. The memorial features the *Gemini 3* spacecraft, photographs, artifacts, and stories from Grissom's life, all aimed at inspiring young Hoosiers.

Armstrong would be the one to fulfill the dreams of the nation. With more than half a billion people watching on television on July 20, 1969, he climbed down a ladder from the *Apollo 11* spacecraft and stepped onto the moon, declaring, "That's one small step for a man, one giant leap for mankind."

Grissom and Chaffee both have halls named in their memory at their alma mater. In 2007 Purdue dedicated a new home for its engineering program in Armstrong's honor. The Neil Armstrong Hall of Engineering houses state-of-the-art equipment and a zero-gravity lab that re-creates the weightlessness and microgravity of space, a technological advantage certain to attract the next generation of space heroes to West Lafayette.

Directions: The Gus Grissom Memorial is near the entrance to Spring Mill State Park, 3333 Indiana 60 East, Mitchell.

Directions: The Neil Armstrong Hall of Engineering is located at Stadium and Northwestern Avenues on Purdue's West Lafayette campus.

PHOTO BY DAVID UMBERGER/PURDUE NEWS SERVICE

A bronze statue of Neil Armstrong greets visitors to the Neil Armstrong Hall of Engineering at Purdue University. The sculpture, by North Carolina artist Chas Fagan, depicts Armstrong as an undergraduate in the 1950s.

BEAN BLOSSOM IS SYNONYM FOR BLUEGRASS IN INDIANA

Before New York had Woodstock, Indiana had Bean Blossom.

It is just a notch in the road to motorists heading south from Indianapolis on Indiana 135 en route to the art colony at Nashville or Brown County State Park.

But to folks who know bluegrass, it's Mecca—home to the nation's oldest, continuously running bluegrass festival. It was launched in 1967 by the legendary singer/mandolin picker Bill Monroe. (Woodstock, a one-time three-day rock 'n roll concert, came two years later.)

"Most Hoosiers have never heard of Bean Blossom, but all the bluegrass people in the world know where it is, and a lot of them come to it," said Jim Peva, historian for Bill Monroe Music Park and Campground and a longtime Monroe friend.

Acclaimed as the "father of bluegrass" in his *New York Times* obituary, Monroe was born in 1911 in Kentucky and spent most of his career in Tennessee, where he performed regularly on Nashville's *Grand Ole Opry*. But his story as a performer really began in Indiana.

At age eighteen, Monroe moved to Whiting to join two of his older brothers working at the Sinclair Oil Refinery. They formed a band that played publicly for the first time on radio stations in Hammond and Gary and performed in traveling country music shows.

The brothers went their separate ways in 1938, liberating Monroe to become "his own man," as biographer Richard D. Smith put it. Monroe put together a new band with a new sound: Bill Monroe and His Blue Grass Boys, from which the genre took its name. The group featured Monroe on the mandolin, singing blues-like solos in high keys with fiddle, guitar, banjo and bass accompaniment.

Sidemen came and went—more than 200 of them over the years—but one in particular contributed to the band's distinctive tone: banjoist Earl Scruggs with his unusual three-finger picking method.

It is not certain when Monroe paid his first visit to Bean Blossom, site of the Brown County Jamboree Barn that had been entertaining locals since 1943. Peva suspects it was 1951, when the Bluegrass Boys were booked to play there. Monroe took an immediate liking to the place and bought it.

The Bean Blossom Bluegrass Festival is the oldest, continuously running bluegrass festival in the world, held every June at the Bill Monroe Music Park and Campground.

Under Monroe's watchful eye and brother Birch's management, Bean Blossom became a bluegrass cultural center, drawing crowds and Opry stars to spring and fall jamborees.

In June 1967 "a new era began at the old park with a modestly advertised but momentous event: Bill Monroe's first bluegrass festival." The event combined top talent, instructional workshops, a Sunday morning gospel service, and a whole lot of jamming in the campground. The inaugural festival lasted two days, was attended by "a few hundred people," and netted Monroe $1,700, according to Thomas A. Adler, author of a 2011 book on Bean Blossom's role in American music history. The festival grew into a weeklong event attracting thousands and became a prototype for bluegrass festivals elsewhere.

Monroe died in 1996 and the facility was sold to businessman Dwight Dillman, who renovated it and dedicated it to Monroe's memory. Campsites are available May through October; the park hosts a half dozen or so events a year, including the June festival, which celebrated its forty-ninth anniversary in 2015.

Adjacent to the campground, a museum displays memorabilia from Monroe's life and from famous acquaintances, including Jimmy Martin and Dolly Parton. The collection includes a piano played by Minnie Pearl and Del Wood in the old Brown County Jamboree Barn.

Directions: Bean Blossom is five miles north of Nashville on Indiana 135.

INDIANAPOLIS STAYED CALM AS NATION BURNED

On April 4, 1968, Indianapolis showed its best self.

Democratic presidential candidate Robert F. Kennedy had come to town to hold a nighttime political rally at Broadway and Seventeenth Streets in a mostly African American neighborhood on the near north side of Indianapolis. Also that night, Mayor Richard G. Lugar was attending a banquet at the Marott Hotel to celebrate Shortridge High School's trip to the state basketball finals. It should have been a festive evening for all concerned, but history intervened.

At 6:05 p.m. Reverend Martin Luther King Jr. was assassinated by a white man as he stood on a balcony outside his motel room in Memphis, Tennessee. More than 100 cities burned with protests that night and in the days to follow, but Indianapolis did not. Many credited Kennedy's presence with defusing a crisis.

Kennedy had learned of the shooting en route from a campaign event in Muncie. Rather than cancel the rally, he decided to discard prepared remarks and speak from the heart. Upon arrival, he saw approximately 2,500 people standing, waving banners. Few were aware of the civil rights leader's death.

Standing on a platform set up on an outdoor basketball court, Kennedy said: "I have some very sad news for all of you ... and that is that Martin Luther King was shot and was killed tonight."

Screams were heard in the audience and cries of "No! No!"

Kennedy continued, "What we need in the United States is not hatred; what we need in the United States is not violence and lawlessness, but is love and wisdom and compassion toward one another."

The speech lasted only a few minutes. Kennedy reminded the crowd that he also had lost someone dear, his brother President John F. Kennedy, to a white man's bullet. He concluded by urging people to go home and say prayers for King's family and the country.

Coincidentally, Kennedy planned to spend the night at the Marott, where the Shortridge basketball dinner took place. Lugar was informed of King's death at the dinner but did not share the news with others. He waited in the lobby after the banquet until he knew Kennedy had arrived safely.

PHOTO BY LARRY LADIG

The Landmark for Peace *memorial depicts Martin Luther King Jr. and Robert F. Kennedy with outstretched arms.*

Lugar asked eyewitnesses how the rally had gone. "They said it was a very beautiful and moving experience, that it had been nonviolent and that people were deeply troubled but did not manifest their grief in other ways," recalled Lugar.

The next morning the mayor got to work. As reports came in of violence across the nation, he called black civic leaders to his office to discuss the city's approach to racial equality issues. He met with concerned residents at neighborhood centers and on street corners.

No one could have foreseen that on June 6, just eighty-five days into his candidacy, Robert Kennedy would suffer the same fate as King. On June 9 Lugar led a memorial service on the plaza of City Hall, noting his admiration for Kennedy's conduct throughout the campaign.

Kennedy's soothing words had kept the peace in the hours immediately following King's death. Mayor Lugar's outreach to African Americans helped keep the peace in the days that followed.

That significant moment in Indianapolis race relations is remembered to this day at King Memorial Park at Seventeenth and Broadway Streets. In 1995 city officials dedicated a *Landmark for Peace* sculpture near the spot where Kennedy announced King's death. The two civil rights leaders are sculpted in bronze, reaching toward each other from two curved panels.

Directions: Martin Luther King Jr. Park is at 1702 North Broadway Street, Indianapolis.

UNIGOV SAVED INDIANAPOLIS'S ECONOMY AND TAX BASE

In the late 1960s, just as the word Rust Belt entered modern vocabulary to describe the Industrial Midwest, Indianapolis devised a bold new strategy for its economic future.

Unigov—short for unified government—was a plan to increase governmental efficiency and halt the erosion of the tax base by merging the city of Indianapolis with the surrounding Marion County.

Conceived by Mayor Richard G. Lugar and other Republican leaders and authorized by the Indiana General Assembly in 1969, Unigov became a national model for dealing with urban blight. In the eyes of many, it saved Indianapolis from the fate of Detroit, Gary, and Toledo, among other struggling cities.

It "laid the foundations for the emergence of the modern Indianapolis," former Mayor William H. Hudnut said in a 2005 interview with the *Indiana Magazine of History*. "Unigov represented a dramatic and successful initiative to reform governance structures in Indianapolis."

The factors setting the stage for Unigov were varied and complex. Prior to Unigov, Marion County was a confusing patchwork of sixty different governing bodies: the county, twenty-three cities and towns, nine townships, eleven school districts, and sixteen special-purpose units such as the Indianapolis Airport Authority. With so many competing entities, it was a challenge to collaborate on issues facing the entire metropolitan area.

The issues covered the spectrum from poverty to a declining industrial base. Linda B. Weintraut, writing in the *Encyclopedia of Indianapolis*, blamed increased mobility after World War II for the decline of central cities. The development of residential subdivisions, shopping malls, and suburban office buildings had all sucked commerce and residents from downtown Indianapolis, which in turn hurt tax collections.

The passage of Unigov stabilized the city budget, restored its AAA bond rating, and led to an outpouring of funds—federal and private—for community and commercial development projects. Some of the most visible were Market Square Arena, home of the Indiana Pacers; a $4.7 million renovation of the City Market; a $46 million Merchants

The twenty-eighth floor observation deck of the Indianapolis City-County building gives visitors a bird's-eye view of the consolidated city.

Plaza hotel-office complex; and the new American United Life Insurance building.

Attorney Eugene Lausch, who headed the Division of Code Enforcement of the new consolidated government, said efficiency in planning and zoning was an immediate benefit, but there were "soft" advantages, too. "It created a sense on the part of people in suburban areas that we were all in this together," he recalled.

Unigov was not a complete consolidation, nor a perfect remedy. For example, it did not combine fire or police departments (the Marion County Sheriff and Indianapolis Police Departments merged in 2005), and it left intact the cities of Lawrence, Beech Grove, Speedway, and Southport. By far the most notable omission was the schools.

The Indianapolis Public Schools Board had preferred a unified school district, but political reality of the time would not allow it. The IPS schools were predominantly black, the township schools mostly white. "To have included schools in Unigov would have raised the specter of racial integration . . . and would have meant instant death for the plan," the Reverend Landrum Shields, IPS school board president, acknowledged at the time.

A year after Unigov took effect, U.S. District Judge S. Hugh Dillin ruled that Indianapolis schools were unlawfully segregated; in 1975 he ordered busing of IPS students to the townships, an action that would have been unnecessary in a consolidated school corporation.

The question is often posed: What would Indianapolis look like today had Unigov not been approved?

A 2014 report, "Forty Years after Unigov" by Jeff Wachter, suggests a very different landscape, both figuratively and literally. Most certainly Indianapolis would be a smaller city with a smaller budget and fewer of the amenities that characterize a vibrant city life.

Directions: The Indianapolis City-County Building is at 200 East Washington Street in downtown Indianapolis.

9/11 ETCHED IN HOOSIERS' MEMORIES

September 11, 2001. The very mention of that date sends chills down the spine of all Hoosiers, indeed all Americans, who lived through it.

It was the day that terrorists from the Middle East turned commercial aircraft into weapons of mass destruction, killing nearly 3,000 people in the World Trade Center, the Pentagon, and on board four hijacked planes.

"It was the first shot in the global war on terrorism," reflected Teri Maude, the widow of one of nine Hoosiers who died that day. Her husband was Lieutenant General Timothy Maude, the highest-ranking general officer to be killed in hostile action since World War II.

Tim Maude was an Indianapolis native who enlisted in the military while a student at Marian University in Indianapolis. After serving in Vietnam in 1967 and 1968, earning a Bronze Star, he opted for a career with the army and never looked back. Along the way, he fell in love with fellow Marian student Teri Campbell; they married and had two daughters.

When American Airlines Flight 77 slammed into the Pentagon, Maude was in a meeting with contractors discussing the military's survivor benefit program. Teri, a civilian army employee, was at a conference in San Diego, where she watched the terrible events unfold on television.

By day's end, although his remains had not been identified, it was clear to Teri and officials in Washington that Tim was among the victims. So were many of their colleagues and friends. "Not only did I suffer personal loss, but my army family took one hell of a hit that day," Maude said. "There was a 27 percent casualty rate in Tim's unit and a 37 percent injury rate."

Maude was one of four Hoosiers killed in the Pentagon attack. The others were Colonel Canfield Boone, Milan; Major Stephen V. Long, Cascade; and Brenda Gibson, Indianapolis, a civilian employee.

Opposite: Two 11,000-pound beams from the Twin Towers are the focal point of the Indianapolis 9/11 Memorial.

In New York City, four Hoosiers who worked in the World Trade Center died when American Airlines Flight 11 and United Airlines Flight 175 hit the North and South Towers. They were: Gary Bright, Muncie; Katie McCloskey, South Bend; Stacy Peak, Tell City; and Karen Juday, Elkhart. Eddie Dillard, raised in Gary, was a passenger on Flight 77 en route to California to visit his son when that plane struck the Pentagon.

The fourth plane, United Airlines Flight 43, crashed in Somerset County, Pennsylvania, after passengers and crew learned about the earlier attacks and attempted to retake the aircraft.

Teri Maude views all the victims as war heroes and says she is glad their sacrifice has been remembered at memorials in Washington, New York, Pennsylvania, and cities across the country, including the Maudes' hometown.

Now living in South Carolina, Teri was in Indianapolis in 2014 to help dedicate a 600-pound slab of Indiana limestone salvaged from the Pentagon's devastation and included in the city's 9-11 memorial on Ohio Street. The memorial features two upright beams from the Twin Towers and a pair of granite walls inscribed with remembrances of 9-11. A life-size sculpture of a bald eagle is perched atop one of the beams, its wings outstretched and eyes looking east.

Teri has visited that memorial and the one at the Pentagon on numerous occasions. "I find these places more a place of reflection than a war monument," she observed. "I get great peace there because it is fulfilling the promise everybody made to each other that day: We will never forget."

Directions: The 9/11 Memorial is at 421 West Ohio Street in Indianapolis.

A BICENTENNIAL GIFT TO HOOSIERS MELTZER WOODS

Eight miles from Shelbyville at a place called Meltzer Woods, a remnant of old-growth forest thrives untouched by human development. It is an oasis of tall trees in the midst of some of the most fertile farmland anywhere.

The forty-eight-acre expanse is a powerful reminder that our history is older than our state. Many of these trees predated the writing of Indiana's 1816 constitution; some are older than the Declaration of Independence.

"I have never been to Meltzer Woods with anybody who was not awestruck by the power of nature," said Cliff Chapman, executive director of the Central Indiana Land Trust that preserves areas such as this on the public's behalf. "Take a walk, and you'll see for yourself."

Meltzer Woods is one of the newest additions to his organization's inventory, an acquisition made possible through a program called the Bicentennial Nature Trust.

In honor of Indiana's two hundredth birthday, Governor Mitch Daniels established the trust in 2012 to protect natural heritage sites at risk of development. The state provided $20 million and Lilly Endowment $10 million to go toward matching grants that communities, government agencies, and nonprofits could leverage to purchase land from willing sellers.

Meltzer Woods was a priority project, Chapman explained, because there is so little old-growth forest left. It is what Indiana looked like before the pioneers—a time when 87 percent of the state was covered with hardwoods, compared to 20 percent in 2015.

The Meltzer family has owned this land since 1857, when John Frederick Meltzer bought 160 acres for farmland. Over decades the farm expanded and today Phil Meltzer and his son-in-law grow soybeans and corn on 280 acres, minus the forest, which they left undisturbed.

In 1973 Meltzer Woods was designated a National Natural Landmark for its "contrasting forest types (beech-maple and lowland mixed forests) and exceptionally large individuals of several tree species."

Slivers of sunlight break through the canopy of old-growth forest at Meltzer Woods.

The family sold the property to the Central Indiana Land Trust at well below market value to make sure future generations would not be tempted to sell it for its timber value.

More than one hundred similar projects across the state have set aside woods, wetlands, and recreational property for the public's enjoyment.

In Gibson and Pike Counties, the Sycamore Land Trust bought 1,043 acres of former surface mine bordering Patoka National Wildlife Refuge. The site includes marsh, forested wetlands, upland forests, prairie plantings, and several lakes.

Lagrange County Parks purchased 109 acres adjacent to its existing Pine Knob Park, featuring a sedge meadow, fen wetlands, and oak/hickory woodland.

Fallen tree trunks and large branches provide shelter and foraging grounds for mammals and insects in old-growth forests.

French Lick in Orange County acquired sixty-eight acres of forest, including two ravines and a pair of seasonal streams that drain into French Lick Creek. The land will become a public park with hiking and mountain-bike trails.

It has taken the better part of our statehood to decide that preservation matters. Our history, after all, is found not just in books and museums but in the world around us. It is in the coal and limestone beneath our feet. It is in the corn growing in our fields. It is in the canals, railroad tracks, and roads that moved us from one part of the state to another as Indiana grew from pioneer past into modernity. It is in the rivers that flow beside us and the trees that tower above us.

Thanks to the Bicentennial Trust and a Hoosier family's foresight, it is also due west of Milroy in a place called Meltzer Woods.

Directions: Meltzer Woods is just north of the intersection of Indiana 244 and 600 East in Shelby County.